T0194569

BIBLICAL SOUL LEADERSHIP

A Revelation *of* God's Word

EPHREM ERMIAS MAMO

WESTBOW
PRESS®
A DIVISION OF THOMAS NELSON
& ZONDERVAN

Scriptures taken from the Holy Bible, New International Version®, NIV®. Copyright © 1973, 1978, 1984, 2011 by Biblica, Inc.™ Used by permission of Zondervan. All rights reserved worldwide. www.zondervan.com The "NIV" and "New International Version" are trademarks registered in the United States Patent and Trademark Office by Biblica, Inc.™

This book is a work of non-fiction. Unless otherwise noted, the author and the publisher make no explicit guarantees as to the accuracy of the information contained in this book and in some cases, names of people and places have been altered to protect their privacy.

WestBow Press books may be ordered through booksellers or by contacting:

WestBow Press
A Division of Thomas Nelson & Zondervan
1663 Liberty Drive
Bloomington, IN 47403
www.westbowpress.com
1 (866) 928-1240

Because of the dynamic nature of the Internet, any web addresses or links contained in this book may have changed since publication and may no longer be valid. The views expressed in this work are solely those of the author and do not necessarily reflect the views of the publisher, and the publisher hereby disclaims any responsibility for them.

Any people depicted in stock imagery provided by Getty Images are models, and such images are being used for illustrative purposes only. Certain stock imagery © Getty Images.

ISBN: 978-1-9736-4860-4 (sc)
ISBN: 978-1-9736-4859-8 (hc)
ISBN: 978-1-9736-4861-1 (e)

Library of Congress Control Number: 2018914747

Print information available on the last page.

WestBow Press rev. date: 01/14/2019

CONTENTS

ACKNOWLEDGMENTS

First, I would like to thank God for His mercy, grace, and love. He bestowed every day of my life on me. I have remained upright because of God's love and kindness. All the glory, honor, and praise belong to the Lord. This book is an act of obedience to God's purpose in my life. His continuous guidance and leadership have made me who I am.

Second, I would like to thank my wife, Rose Mamo, for supporting me through prayer and encouragement. She has been an incredible wife and helper. God has taught me a lot through her, and I am thankful God brought us together.

Third, I would like to thank my parents, Dr. Ermias Mamo and Amarech Milikyas Mamo, for their prayers and encouragement. God brought us to America from a nomadic land in southern Ethiopia. Our journey was not easy, but God's eternal grace kept us steady.

Finally, I am thankful for my relatives in Ethiopia and my wife's family in America for their encouraging words. Prophet Ermias Balcha, apostle Belete, pastor Bill, and the Wood Village Baptist community have been a great support system and body of Christ.

INTRODUCTION

Everyone on Earth is precious to God whether we believe it or not. In my life, I have made many mistakes that I regret. I made those mistakes because I was lost and didn't know who to turn to. I came to realize that my greatest hope was Jesus and decided to put all my hope and trust in Him. That decision helped me grow as a young man and led me to write a book that encouraged positive transformation through Jesus Christ.

Life does not always turn out the way we want it to, and the question is "Why?" The answer is in this book's title: *Biblical Soul Leadership*. As Christians, we were raised to believe that if we were Christians, then everything would and should be perfect. Parents, churches, and communities didn't know how to explain what it meant to be a Christian, because they were never clearly taught by their own parents.

Now, whose fault is it? Nobody's. As believers, we need to continuously seek God and be transformed by Him. True transformation begins with knowing the truth. When regarding the Pharisees, Jesus tells His disciples, "If the blind lead the blind, both will fall into a pit" (Matthew 15:14 NIV). In other words, your faith should focus not on the church, theology, or Christian leaders but the finished work of Christ. *Biblical Soul Leadership* focuses on making Jesus Christ the foundation of our faith and defining the soul according to the word of

God. Its teaching are necessary because parents, churches, and communities haven't been teaching their congregation about the combined power of Christ and the soul.

Many churches and communities talk about the power of Christ, which is important, but they don't apply power to the soul. In this book, the soul will be explained in a simple structure. Many Christians have the power of Christ, but they do not know how to apply it.

There are many movies with superheroes who have superpowers. What if the superheroes did not know how to use their superpowers? Their enemies would hurt them and destroy their lives. Many Christians are like that. So, how do we learn to use our superpowers? By understanding every aspect of the soul.

The word "soul" has lost its real meaning. Many individuals will say they know Jesus, but they live a defeated life full of fear, loss, lust, addiction, and depression. As a result, many negative questions arise. Why don't I experience the victory of Christ? Why do I feel like a loser? Why am I always angry with God? Why is life empty? Is God even real? If God is real, why do I have so much pain and sorrow in my life? Now that I am a Christian, why do I suffer more than unbelievers? Is God perfect? Is God's word reliable? The questions go on. We all have asked at least one of these questions at one time or another, and that's okay. God always rescued us.

In Hebrew, the word for soul is *nephesh*, which is translated as a "soul, living being, life, self, person, desire, passion, appetite, emotion." This definition is so broad it's confusing. The Greek word for soul is *psuché*, which is translated as "the vital breath, breath of life, the human soul, the soul as the seat of affections and will, the self, a human person, an individual." It's essential to understand the simple definition. Why write a book if a simple definition is available? The answer is simple: understanding the definition of a soul is not enough to transform individuals and nations. The word "soul" needs a revelation from God in order to transform and deliver humanity. Many authors who have written about the soul have had great resources, information, and knowledge, but they haven't grabbed their readers' attention.

Many Christians define themselves as people who were called to live in misery without a victory, but John 16:33 states, "I have told you these things, so that in me you may have peace. In this world, you will have trouble. But take heart! I have overcome the world" (NIV). Many believers have misunderstood and misinterpreted this verse, focusing on the trouble instead of the fact that we can overcome the trouble. We have heard many sermons attempt to explain victory through Christ, but they and God's people need a prophetic revelation based on the word of God. God has given me a prophetic revelation to share with the world regarding how to live a victorious life through Christ. We all have seen trouble, but now it is time to experience victory.

After studying the definition of the soul, I have determined a more reliable and accurate version similar to the Greek and Hebrew, and I have categorized it into several parts. The first category is called the major soul, which consists of our thoughts. It's called the major soul not because it's more important but because it is the foundation and driving force of humanity. The second category is called the minor soul (emotion, will, body, and action), because it follows the major soul in everything. The third category chapter three, four, and five are called the soul's influential spirits. These potent spirits are human nature, the Holy Spirit, and Lucifer's Spirit (a spirit that is focused on negativity, mixes lies and truth, and manipulates), and they exist in the major soul. The final category is focused on understanding salvation.

This book will explain each of the categories in detail. It's critical that we understand how these components impact our daily lives. A thorough understanding of the soul will help resolve every one of our sins, struggle, doubts, and fears.

This book will focus on discovering the soul and finding victory in Christ. Before we begin, let us do a short prayer:

Heavenly Father, you have changed my life through your word and the revelation you have given me. I pray you would touch someone's life and reveal your victory in them. As they read this book, I pray that their desire to pray, read the Bible, and submit to you would increase. God, it is by your mercy, grace, and undeserving love that I wrote this book. I am nothing without you, but when you came into my life, I became somebody, a child of God. I received my revelation from reading your book, the Bible. Please give every individual a revelation and deeper understanding of you. God, many of my brothers and sisters have been experiencing the troubling aspects of Christianity, but from this moment on, help them discover its victory. This book is not an attempt to replace the Bible, because your word remains forever (1 Peter 1:25 NIV). Instead, it is a reminder that you have a profound revelation for all your children, so that they may experience victory through your son, Jesus Christ. Father, I pray that our lives would be ones of repentance, submission, and humility. Thank you for your mercy, grace, and eternal love. In Jesus's name, amen.

CHAPTER ONE:
MAJOR SOUL
(THOUGHT)

Thought is the first component of the major soul, because it is the reason the soul begins and functions. What is a thought? It is an idea or opinion that creates a reality based on a spiritual foundation. Every thought comes from a spiritual foundation, whether we want to be aware of it or not. Before Adam and Eve sinned, humanity only had one spiritual foundation: God. But after they sinned (Genesis 3 NIV), two more spiritual foundations—darkness and human nature (Genesis 2:17 NIV)—attacked humanity in order to enter its soul.

A thought can be a word, image, idea, story, circumstance, event, hurt, fantasy, pride, or concept that tries to come alive. Thoughts have only three sources: human nature, the Holy Spirit, and Lucifer's Spirit. It is vital to know where thoughts originate so they can be led in the right direction. Society's medical science definition for thought is "Cerebrum an enlarged anterior or upper part of the brain; especially: the expanded anterior portion of the brain that in higher mammals overlies the rest of the brain, consists of cerebral hemispheres and connecting structures, and is considered to be the seat of conscious mental processes" (Merriam-Webster Dictionary). This book focuses on thought from a spiritual perspective.

A thought is like a seed that wants to live and grow. A thought can develop and become a lifestyle—I call it *thought germination*. The word "germination" is not only used for plant development but anything that comes into existence. Our thoughts come alive when we put them into action. What is inside a thought? Ideas, assumptions, information, imagination, interpretation, and past experiences. These components blossom based on how much a person considers a particular thought.

A thought is always hungry for a spiritual source. When an individual focuses on one spiritual source, his or her thoughts grow quickly. When a thought grows quickly, it becomes a belief. A seed sprouts and grows when it receives moisture, warmth, and nutrients from water and sunlight. At that moment, a plant's roots strengthen. When one of the spiritual sources fully supports a thought, faith and belief develop.

Faith and belief move from the major soul (thought) to the minor soul (emotion, will, body, and action) and reveal the influential spirits (human nature, the Holy Spirit, and Lucifer's Spirit). Adam and Eve had perfect thoughts at first, because they had one spiritual source: God. When they ate from the tree of the knowledge of good and evil (Genesis 3:6), they added human nature and the devil's attack (Lucifer's Spirit) to their spiritual sources, resulting in the three influential spirits. God left the soul at that moment, and humanity was left with their human nature and the devil's attack (Lucifer's Spirit). In spite of humanity's sins, God showed His eternal love to humanity through Christ.

The Fall of Humanity and Thought (Genesis 3 NIV)

The story of Adam, Eve, and the serpent (Genesis 3) is a good example of a thought being attacked. The devil constantly targets our thoughts, because they are one of the greatest weapons that God blessed us with. If the devil can control our thoughts, he can control everything in our lives. The devil wants to destroy humanity's relationship with God. As a friend at church once told me, the devil works a lot of overtime. The devil's joy and delight is to see humanity walk away from God. Before the devil tricked Eve, he first examined her thought process. For example, in order to build a stable house, its foundation has to be strong. A house will fall right away if it has a weak foundation. Our thoughts are like a house in need of a strong foundation. Their foundation is Christ, but they easily fall because of sin.

The devil wanted to destroy Eve's foundation, so he struck her thoughts. He wanted to separate her from God and fill her life with sin so he could control her. He started with a question, "Did God really say, 'You must not eat from any tree in the garden'?" (Genesis 3:1 NIV). Why did he begin with a question? Because it's the best way to capture people's attention and get them talking. The devil picked a topic that was vital to Eve: food and its resources. Since food is essential for humans, the devil knew he could get to her thoughts. More often than not, the devil uses things that are important to us to make our lives miserable. In Adam and Eve's case, he used food.

Once the devil's question captured her attention, Eve started having an unnecessary conversation with him. This was Eve's biggest mistake. Both she and the devil knew what the Lord had commanded in regards to the tree of the knowledge of good and evil, but the devil pretended to forget the decree in order to deceive Eve. He knew the command, because he otherwise wouldn't have asked a question about which tree to eat from. The devil's deception began the moment Eve responded. Our thoughts are often questioned by the devil (to frighten), ourselves (for earthly comfort), or God (for repentance). Various outcomes can occur depending on who we choose to respond to.

Eve reminds the devil of God's command and instruction, but the devil's heart was not open to the truth—he had no desire to obey it. Eve's willingness to respond to the devil's question was an attempt to make him accept and believe the truth (Genesis 3:2-3 NIV). We live in a generation where many pastors and church leaders try to save people using Eve's method of forcing the Bible and religious activity. Eve had the right idea, but it was done in the wrong way.

What could she have done better? She could have asked God how to deal with the serpent. Going to God is not easy, otherwise Eve would have done it. Many church leaders and pastors neglect going to God, making decisions based on their reading, degree, or position. We must change the way we think and lead by prioritizing God.

What would happen if Eve went to God before responding to the serpent? What if Adam had stopped the conversation and told Eve to talk to God first? Both Adam and Eve were at fault. Both were equally wrong. We learn from them that their refusal to go to God, and their attempt to take on the devil under their own willpower, brought disaster and suffering for all of humanity.

The way we think and the decisions we make often affect our marriages, families, communities, churches, counties, states, countries, and the world at large. What begins in our thoughts can bless or curse this world. Humanity is always thinking about something. As children and believers, we must redirect our thoughts to God or we will be in trouble. God gave us the gift of thought when He breathed the breath of life (Genesis 2:7 NIV). "Thinking"—or the major soul, as I call it—was created so we could have a relationship with God and live for His glory.

After Eve tried to remind the devil of the truth, the devil responded, "You will not certainly die. . . For God knows that when you eat from it your eyes will be opened, and you will be like God, knowing good and evil" (Genesis 3:4-5 NIV). Since the devil's response was something other than the truth, Adam and Eve should have fled, but the couple stayed and became open-minded.

The devil not only twisted the truth but also gave Adam and Eve false hope. This was his plan:

1. Find what was important to Adam and Eve (e.g., food, tree)
2. Ask a question that would motivate Eve to talk
3. Tempt Eve to rely on her own will rather than God's
4. Twist the truth
5. Give false hope
6. Imply that God is a liar

The Bible does not say much about Adam, but we do know that he was with Eve (Genesis 3:6 NIV). Adam may not have said anything aloud, but he did say a lot with his silence. His quietness indicated that he agreed with Eve and the serpent, because he later ate the apple alongside his wife.

I call Adam's response *defeated leadership*. He had the opportunity to intervene and protect his marriage, but he gave in instead. Almost all sin can be avoided or overcome. The problem with humanity is that we say too much and fall, or we say too little and still fall.

So, what do we do? We seek the Lord. Seeking the Lord does not begin at church or during devotion time, it starts in our minds. Humanity has the opportunity to lead its thoughts toward God 24 hours a day, seven days a week, and 365 days a year. There is no room to complain about life, because we have a weapon (Jesus Christ) that makes a difference.

Eve and the devil had a standoff (decision making) until she and Adam gave in to sin. "When the woman saw that the fruit of the tree was good for food and pleasing to the eye, and also desirable for gaining wisdom, she took some and ate it. She also gave some to her husband, who was with her, and he ate it" (Genesis 3:6 NIV). Adam and Eve had been defeated in their thought process before they had eaten the fruit.

I once found an interesting television show that captured my attention. It distracted me from my chores, school, and homework, and I slowly realized that the show was controlling my life. The devil uses a similar method to trap us. People don't typically fall into sin, they slide into immorality. The devil makes us slide before we fall. Sin is not an ugly monster with big horns, it is attractive and desirable. This aspect of sin is not talked about in the church. If sin were always ugly, the whole planet would be holy. It is the result of sin that's ugly, and the process is instant gratification. Thinking about the consequences of sin can shed light on the way we think about sin and make decisions.

"Then the eyes of both of them were opened, and they realized they were naked; so they sewed fig leaves together and made coverings for themselves" (Genesis 3:7 NIV). This verse refers to the moment we realize we disobeyed God. Most of us have experienced shame and disappointment, and it all started in our thought process. There is always hope in Christ, because He is prepared to deliver us from sin. Humanity feels shame because God did not create us to live in sin but to experience growth and victory in Christ.

Murder and the Thought Process (Genesis 4 NIV)

Cain murdered his brother, Abel, because of jealousy. Before he did, God said to him, "Why are you angry? Why is your face downcast? If you do what is right, will you not be accepted? But if you do not do what is right, sin is crouching at your door; it desires to have you, but you must rule over it" (Genesis 4:6–7 NIV). The Lord questioned Cain because He wanted him to examine his thinking. God favored Abel's offering, and that angered Cain. His anger began in his thoughts, and it rapidly turned into rage. His emotions were unexamined, so God tried to calm him down. God often does the same in our lives to help us reexamine our motives. Sin and evil spirits wait for us to mess up at all times. Cain responded to the sinful thought instead of rebuking it, and it cost him his brother. Sin has a cost, so we must rule over it, trust God, and rely on His grace.

Abel's offering was accepted and favored because he brought the best fat portions from the firstborn of his flock to the Lord (Genesis 4:4 NIV). Humans think about having the best life on Earth, so they offer leftovers to God. Abel was different. He brought the best to God. God examined both Abel and Cain's hearts and favored Abel. God absolutely deserves our best gift; therefore, we must give God what he deserves. In our thoughts, we must believe and know that God always deserves the best. God, our creator, has done so much in our lives. It is beyond imagining. Abel understood how much God meant to him. He appreciated God's mercy, blessing, and protection in his life. Modern Abel would be someone who spends time with God, repents, and relies on God's grace. Just as God examined Abel and Cain, He will test us.

The biggest question for us to ask concerns the kind of thought life we want to have. Are we like Abel or Cain? Based on the type of offerings they presented, Cain kept the best for himself. Many individuals who live for themselves do not respect God or prioritize Him. Cain allowed his human nature to do all of the thinking for him, and the human nature focuses on the self. When we allow human nature to be in charge, it will do anything to make itself happy. Cain killed his brother because he let his human nature control him. Cain was angry with his brother, so he killed him to satisfy his anger. We must be careful not to allow our human nature to dictate our lives.

Abel was a humble servant who prioritized God first. When he gave his best fat portions, he put God above his own wants and needs. Abel stayed close to God and offered him the best. Our minds and thinking processes need to submit to God. Abel's decision to offer the best to God started in his thoughts. The person we choose to become originates in our minds. God blesses our lives so that we will live a life that glorifies Him.

Awareness is one of the best methods for training our minds. The difference between Cain and Abel was awareness and godly thinking. Cain was unaware of his thought process, because he focused on self-happiness. Unawareness of self can lead to horrific action. If Cain had been aware of his thoughts and their consequences, he would not have murdered his brother. Abel was aware of his thought process, and he chose wisely. God calls us to think according to His word and to offer the best of ourselves to Him.

Rape and the Thinking Process (Genesis 34 NIV)

"Now Dinah, the daughter Leah had borne to Jacob, went out to visit the women of the land. When Shechem son of Hamor the Hivite, the ruler of that area, saw her, he took her and raped her" (Genesis 34:1-2 NIV). Why did he rape her? What was his thought process? This was a brutal crime against an innocent person. The Bible does not mention Shechem's thought process, just his action and crime, but his thought process is evident. Shechem lusted over Dinah. His lust began in his thoughts just by looking at her. We don't know Shechem's history, but he may have struggled with this behavior in secret at a young age.

Lewd conduct has been a problem for humanity for centuries. Sexual addiction, rape, adultery, and sexual immorality are still massive problems in our society and the church. In this technological generation, television, movies, pornography, and adult films are rapidly growing and controlling the minds of men and women. Sexual immorality is a huge stumbling block for our marriages, relationships with God, and other things as well.

Why do we see rape, divorce, and sexual addiction in society? To find these answers, we must look at families and their practices. Let's answer the question of why people have children. Married families are terrific and beautiful, but the problem is that people don't have a good reason to have children. Every couple has a different purpose regarding childbirth, such as loneliness, accidents, unplanned pregnancies, traditional expectations, relative's expectations, and the list goes on. Whether we have children for the right or wrong reason, we are responsible for them. Society suffers at times because of irresponsible parents who bring pain to their children and the world.

There are men and women who abandon their children for whatever reason. When their children turn out to be rapists or criminals, they're shocked. If we don't water our plants, they will most likely die. If parents don't take care of their children, they shouldn't be surprised if their children turn out differently than they thought they would. Some parents are so caught up in their career and fame that they assume their children will turn out well without guidance, mentorship, and love. I call that denial and lazy parenting. If people are going to buy a flower and never water it, then they shouldn't buy it in the first place. In other words, if you can't take care of something, don't commit to it.

So what does this have to do with rape and thinking? Everything. How we're raised determines our values. Some people might say I was a good parent, but my child still turned out immoral and criminal? If I was a responsible parent, then it would not be my fault. If I consistently abandoned, mistreated, and neglected my child, then it would be my fault. Let's change the world by modeling godliness and positively influencing children to think wisely.

From Dinah and Shechem's story, we learn that sexual sin and crime still exist today. What controls this generation's men and women and puts them in bondage? Pornography. The problem lies with our thoughts because of visual exposure and other factors. I am not going to talk about its history and medical views of pornography, but I will give a solution for victory: changing our thought processes and practicing godliness.

Let's list the factors that lead to pornography:

1. Television exposure
2. Internet exposure
3. Exposure through friends
4. Insecurity
5. Pleasure
6. Wants
7. Needs

8. Loneliness
9. Society

Regardless of the factor an individual is in, he or she must first discover what his or her values and foundation are in life. Once people know their values and foundation, they can answer whether pornography is right or wrong. For a child of God, it is wrong (Matthew 5:28 NIV). If a Christian looks at a man or woman lustfully, they have committed adultery in their heart; in other words, it is a sin.

The word of God is our solution. Pornography addiction is broken by changing the way we think. How do we do that?

1. Admit that pornography is a sin
2. Admit that it is wrong
3. Ask God for forgiveness
4. Ask God for help and deliverance
5. Read the Bible
6. Pray
7. Worship God with songs and obedience

These are the most important steps, but the list goes on:

8. Attend a church
9. Be part of a church Bible study, prayer group, or other spiritual group
10. If married, give wife quality time
11. If a parent, give children quality time
12. If single, surround one's self with a godly environment, friends, and body of Christ
13. Serve when possible, but prioritize God, marriage, and children first

These are basic yet foundational for spiritual growth. This next list will help those who watch and are addicted to pornography understand how to have a godly view of men and women.

1. Men, if you're married, all other women are your sisters, daughters, and mothers. "Older women as mothers, and younger women as sisters, with absolute purity" (1 Timothy 5:2 NIV).
2. Women, if you're married, all other men are your brothers, sons, and fathers.
3. Young men and old men, if you are single, only one woman will be your wife when the time is right. The rest will be your sisters, daughters, and mothers.
4. Girls and women, if you are single, one man will be your husband, and the rest will be your brothers, sons, and fathers.

Reread the list, and then write the four perspectives on a piece of paper and train your thoughts to view things based on them. Unless you can accept the four perspectives, you will never be delivered from addiction. The thirteen listed elements are critical to the four perspectives. As believers, we must follow and consider everything on these lists. If they become part of our lives, we will walk toward growth, deliverance, and victory.

Thinking and the Human Heart (Genesis 6:5)
"The Lord saw how great the wickedness of the human race had become on the earth, and that every inclination of the thoughts of the human heart was only evil all the time" (Genesis 6:5 NIV). Once Adam and Eve sinned, wickedness

14

increased. When the devil succeeded, Adam and Eve's natures were contaminated by sin (Genesis 3 NIV). Before the fall of men, there were two kinds of natures: godly nature and human nature. The godly nature was focused on glorifying God in everything (1 Corinthians 10:31 NIV). It was never contaminated until sin. Before the fall, Adam and Eve had a godly nature, and there was no shame because of it (Genesis 2:25 NIV). The couple walked close to God, and they were in His perfect will.

Their sin released an outbreak that affected the entire human race like a disease. This disease, sin, was contagious and dangerous. It was like a fire that started out small and then multiplied. Some fires are so big that they destroy homes, people, and everything else nearby. The best way to put out a fire is to deal with it while it's small. Sin can be stopped if we know how to deal with it. So, how do we do that?

1. We must trust that God's ways are perfect (Psalm 18:30 NIV)
2. We must change how we think (Philippians 4:8 NIV) and fight the battles in our thoughts
3. We must continue to seek God and walk toward righteousness, holiness, and submission to God's will (Matthew 6:33 NIV)

Sin put human nature in charge, but there is hope for victory in Christ. Trusting God, changing our thinking, and continuously seeking God is the foundation of victory. When humanity discovers its true self, it realizes that life is terrifying to live without God. Many individuals are addicted to drugs, drinking, pornography, etc., because sin is addictive if we don't deal with it.

The hearts and thoughts of humanity are wicked apart from

God, but what about atheists who do good? Many atheists have no clue that the good in them is from God. Anyone alive and breathing is blessed by God. He is the reason for life. Whether we believe it or not, everyone carries the gift of God's breath (Genesis 2:7 NIV). It is almost impossible to be apart from God since we carry His gift. Some people are determined to deny God until they die, but everything we have is from God. Why not honor that gift and live for Him?

Adultery, Murder, and Thinking (2 Samuel 11)

A man after God's own heart committed adultery and murder. At times in his life king David lived comfortably because his army won wars without him. "One evening, David got up from his bed and walked around the roof of the palace" (2 Samuel 11:2 NIV).

Let's examine King David's behavior and thought process. He walked around the roof for whatever reason, and until that point, he had not sinned. It was normal to go to the roof for some fresh air, but the king did not stop there. Something else caught his eye: a woman bathing (2 Samuel 11:2 NIV).

Instead of walking away, King David stayed and watched, and then he sent someone to find out more about her; in other words, he stumbled across something unexpected and trapped himself. So many men come across an advertisement, and instead of changing the channel, they stay and watch. King David committed adultery in his heart (Matthew 5:28 NIV), and then took it further by sleeping with her (2 Samuel 11:4 NIV) and killing her husband (2 Samuel 11:15 NIV). Because he looked where he shouldn't have, severe disaster and chaos occurred.

"The eye is the lamp of the body. If your eyes are healthy, your whole body will be full of light. But if your eyes are unhealthy, your whole body will be full of darkness. If then the light within you is darkness, how great is that darkness!" (Matthew 6:22-23 NIV). The eye has the power to influence the mind. Adam and Eve ate the fruit because it was pleasing to the eye. King David stayed on the roof for the same reason. They were all wrong. Adam, Eve, and David could have walked away, but they stayed to enjoy sin instead.

The eye is not holy. It can influence thought, but it is thought that makes the final decision. The eye is just a follower of thought. King David could have left the roof, and Adam and Eve could have walked away from the serpent, but they didn't, because sin deteriorated their thought processes. It weakened their ability to examine and stand by the truth.

Sin's enemies are holiness, righteousness, and obedience to God. Sometimes sin leads us to make a fast decision, causing us to avoid an examination and ignore going to God. The situation was avoidable, but because Adam, Eve, and King David were human, they failed. We all have sinned and fallen short of the glory of God (Romans 3:23 NIV). Does this mean that it's okay to continue to mess up? No, because God has given us everything for a victorious life. When it comes to spiritual battles, it is best to fight in the thought process with God's help. An individual has a significant advantage when the battle occurs in their thoughts instead of their emotions and actions.

Victory happens when we allow God to be in charge. When God is in charge, He encourages us to examine our decisions and faith (2 Corinthians 13:5 NIV). God embolden us to pause on everything in life so we will choose Him and security. Pausing is an excellent method for examining our thoughts; therefore, we need to practice it. Before we allow anything into our lives, we need to pause and think. If a believer pauses, they can examine and be redirected toward the truth.

Pausing and thinking require that we strengthen our foundation, which comes from spending time with God. Pausing and thinking mean nothing without a foundation. The enemy is not beaten by pausing and thinking but by our reliance on the grace of God, who is our foundation. Only then will we make great decisions and be secure in Him.

Solomon's Thinking on Relationships (1 King 11)

One of the wisest men in history, well known for his ability to think effectively, failed to follow in the ways of God. "Solomon's wisdom was greater than the wisdom of all the people of the East, and greater than all the wisdom of Egypt" (1 King 4:30 NIV). How can a man as wise as Solomon stray from God? The Lord commanded His people, the Israelites, to not intermarry with other nations (1 King 11:1-2 NIV). Solomon did not care, however, and married foreign women. Wisdom and foundation in Christ go together. Because of his selfish, sinful desire, Solomon disobeyed God, who was his foundation. Solomon's wisdom was from God, which was given to him to glorify God. When Solomon disobeyed God, he lost the purpose of his wisdom. Humanity can have wisdom without God. A purpose is a powerful weapon that gives individuals meaning and joy in life.

One of the reasons he may have abandoned God was that his wealth and love for women surpassed his desire to obey God. God made Solomon the wisest man alive, but Solomon walked away from Him anyway. Solomon's thoughts got him in trouble when he started to think about his life without God in it; pride and pleasure became his greatest weaknesses. Later on, Solomon said that chasing earthly things was like chasing after the wind (Ecclesiastes 1:14 NIV). He realized that having wisdom, power, wealth and a thousand wives could not fulfill him. In fact, wealth and power caused Solomon to become disobedient and prideful. He ignored God, which is the same as denying Him.

We often think that wealth and earthy pleasure will fulfill us, but they won't. It is better to be poor with God than have significant wealth without God. At times, we ignore God and push Him aside until we need Him; we reject Him and use Him as a tool. We may not realize it, but that hurts God. Instead of disrespecting Him, let us honor Him with our thoughts.

King Manasseh (2 Chronicles 33)

King Manasseh angered God on purpose. Manasseh became king at the young age of 12 (2 Chronicles 33:1 NIV), and he was one of the worst leaders in the Bible. "He did evil in the eyes of the LORD, following the detestable practices of the nations the Lord had driven out before the Israelites" (2 Chronicles 33:2 NIV). His lousy leadership was the result of his thought process. He spent time thinking about everything he did to his nation. Why are evil leaders in charge? Because people allow wicked leaders to destroy and separate them from God. Some leaders, good or bad, represent the majority of people's hearts. Other leaders lie and misuse their authority to take advantage of the people. Leadership problems occur when our thought processes are not focused on God.

To have good leadership in a nation, Christ must be the cornerstone. Many leaders' foundations are based on self, race, money, winning, power, and fame. All of these are wrong and explain why many leaders are hated, though there are leaders that are admired, respected, and honored.

All leaders struggle with sin, which causes permanent

damage to society and their communities if we don't deal with them. Many leaders want to be right all of the time instead of responsible for their action. We need leaders who admit their mistakes and learn from them.

God punished King Manasseh by allowing the King of Assyria to take him as prisoner (2 Chronicles 33:11). After his punishment, Manasseh asked God for forgiveness, and God returned him to his kingdom. What changed Manasseh's thought process? As a prisoner, he had time to examine his leadership. He realized that his thoughts had gotten him in trouble and he needed to fix them (2 Chronicles 33:12, NIV). God saw the change in Manasseh's thinking, so He listened to his prayer and responded positively; thus, King Manasseh returned from prison as a leader who obeyed God's instruction (2 Chronicles 33:15-17 NIV).

Thinking is like the internet: it has a lot of garbage amongst the good, therefore we must examine it. To examine it adequately, we need to build our foundation in Christ, His word, and the Holy Spirit. My prayer for everyone is that we would use our thoughts for the glory of God (1 Corinthians 10:31 NIV). The major soul can affect our lives in a tremendous way, therefore we must take care of it. Taking care of the major soul will allow us to manage the minor soul.

CHAPTER TWO: MINOR SOUL

The minor soul follows our thoughts and is a powerful weapon. It is minor not because it is unimportant but because it acts as a follower. The minor soul consists of emotion, will, action, body, and lifestyle, which are not to be ignored, as they are crucial to our thoughts. They lie between major soul and faith and are essential factors in our daily lives. They are a gift from God and must be used with wisdom, knowledge and guidance from the Holy Spirit.

Emotion

Emotion is a feeling that results from our thinking process's willingness to accept an idea. When the mind ponders an idea, it evokes, stirs up, and heads toward emotion. Based on our thought process and ideology, an eruption of emotions and feelings arise. If our thought process is negative, then our emotions are negative, and if our thought process is positive, then our emotions are positive. Once a thought turns into an emotion, it becomes extremely difficult to examine. Now is the time to examine and control emotion, as we know not all emotions are healthy for humanity. Some emotions— like suicide, depression, and extreme anger—can damage our lives.

Emotion is like hitting the accelerator. When it is out of control, we need to pause and examine it, but we like to react to everything without searching for the truth. Every emotion can be explained and understood in time. For example, when a person feels angry, immediate retaliation typically follows. Once a person is angry, he or she has a limited amount of time before they react. During that limited time, people should remove themselves from the environment. Doing so will help a person cool down and examine the situation.

Negative emotion is like a hungry lion in a cage. Once it's free, the lion will be ready to devour anything it sees. We have positive, negative, and mixed emotion in our mind. Based on the situation, we feel one of these emotions, and the way we express and deal with them can affect our lives and future. Many people struggle with negative emotion, but they never struggle with positive emotion.

Fear and emotion (2 Timothy 1:7)

"For the Spirit God gave us does not make us timid, but gives us power, love and self-discipline" (2 Timothy 1:7 NIV). God did not give us a spirit of fear because fear is a result of the fall (Genesis 3:6 NIV). The devil uses humanity's hurts and weaknesses to encourage fear. Ever since the fall of Adam and Eve, fear has been humanity's greatest weakness. Many people are timid and fearful, which are negative and destructive to self. God gave us power, love, and self-discipline, so the devil attacks us with fear, hate, and lust, because humanity can be corrupted by the opposite of what God has given.

Fear makes many people focus on their hurts and mistakes instead of their power and confidence. I was fearful as a child because of the pain and suffering I experienced. As I grew older, the devil used my pain to trap me in fear until God set me free. God intended for us to be driven by love, but because of sin and the devil, we live in a hateful society.

Hate affects all aspects of our nation: politics, religion, education, etc. It is a disease that humanity ignores. Brain cancer is deadly, and those who are lucky have it for five years—even less in some cases. My point is that cancer ends life while hate lasts a lifetime. Wars are a result of hatred. Many people and leaders do not want to acknowledge this. In life, we avoid dealing with hate, and that leads to self-destruction. When a racist comment is made, society allows it to be a common saying or small mistake instead of identifying it as hate.

Whether it's a racist comment or a hidden disease, we must fight and defeat hate with love. People may live with hate for 70 years, but the heart is too rotten to change. People with rotten hearts hate living, and they always have regrets. Hate destroys the human soul. God won humanity's hearts with His love: His greatest weapon. If individuals, families, communities, states, and nations practiced love, our world would be a better and safer place.

Love is an emotion that focuses on doing the right thing. It seeks peace and resolution. It is God's greatest weapon, but humanity chooses to keep love as its last option. Funny how God's first option is love and humanity's never is.

"Love is patient, love is kind. It does not envy, it does not boast, it is not proud. It does not dishonor others, it is not self-seeking, it is not easily angered, it keeps no record of wrongs. Love does not delight in evil but rejoices with the truth. It always protects, always trusts, always hopes, always perseveres. Love never fails" (1 Corinthians 13:4-8 NIV). Scripture's definitions for love can be seen in our emotions.

Humanity will do anything for temporary, earthly riches while refusing to practice God's lasting and eternal love. God's love is available to everyone when they accept Jesus into their heart and submit to His ways. God is concerned about our thoughts and emotions. Everyone is capable of love, but most don't choose love as a solution.

If anyone is confused about what love means, reread 1 Corinthians 13:4–8. This section of the chapter focuses on emotion, but love can be a thought, action, and lifestyle as well. The soul's power is emotion while its foundation is thought. If we, Christians, want to experience the power of God, we must practice love. Hate only shows others how much we have walked away from God.

Emotion and Self-Discipline

No matter how successful we want to be, we cannot avoid emotion. It is the foundation of motivation. Why do teenagers join gangs? Why does teen pregnancy exist? Why do people give up their future for love? The answer is emotion. Our emotions are powerful enough to change our future in an instant. Many couples love each other at the beginning of their marriages, but they resolve their emotional hurts with divorce. Nobody gets married for divorce, yet divorce is a common reality. We should not judge those who are divorced, but we should find a solution. Divorce, teen pregnancy, gang problems, etc. are a result of emotion, the most sensitive part of humanity. When a man and woman's emotions are hurt, they retaliate and use violence, resulting in separation and hate. It's not rocket science to say that emotions are powerful.

Emotional pain is just like physical pain, as they both depend on an incident. The incident defines the level of emotional and physical pain. People struggle with large amounts of emotional pain. I have never heard of people struggling with positive ones. Nobody has ever come to their parents, society, or God complaining because they were happy. The more people deal with negative emotion, the more they'll gain positive outcome. Negative emotions are like workouts to lose weight or build muscle. They are not easy, as they take commitment, patience, and consistency. Emotion requires exercises of examination, patience, and reexamination of self.

Everyone works to be paid and have a better life. Working on our emotion will allow us to parent, do our work, lead, and mentor others. People don't want to deal with their emotions because it's hard. Doing the hard thing is called self-discipline. Without self-discipline, our society will remain in chaos. All of the world's problems are a result of uncontrolled emotion, and they have solutions, but we refuse to enact them.

Humanity and Emotion

I worked with children for ten years, and their problems were always based on emotion. Many children are emotionally damaged, and society suffers as a result. Parents refuse to take responsibility for their action. They replace their children (and marriage) with careers, education, money, and fame, because they do not know how to deal with themselves. Individuals who were hurt in their childhood and personal life are often unfit to deal with reality. Irresponsible individuals are insecure and full of shame from mistakes in their past, and they constantly try to prove to humanity that they are worthy of love and admiration. We must help those suffering from hidden emotional damage. Irresponsible people are deeply wounded, and they usually avoid dealing with their hurt. The most dangerous thing in life is an unwillingness to deal with the truth. Avoiding the truth puts us in a position to damage those around us, whether consciously or unconsciously.

Parents are not the problem, because they are just as lost as everybody else. Schools, churches, and communities need to teach people how to deal with their hidden feelings and hurts. Many of us find healing by simply being aware of our hidden wounds. Once we are, it's time to write them down and investigate. Write down every factor that negatively affects the way you parent, teach, work, and live your life. Afterwards, reread the list and make one section for factors that cause negativity and a second for solutions to each factor. There is power in writing things down. It helps us grow into a wise and godly person.

Almost all of us attended some kind of class or school, and we usually learned from something that was written down. In today's world, many of us spend thousands of dollars on education, but we rarely write things down to examine, investigate, and better ourselves. I challenge you and myself to write down our hidden emotional issues and investigate solutions.

Will (decision making)

The will is a part of the soul that appear once emotion is under control. Controlled emotion is a dominating thought that can be negative or positive. Thought allows emotion, and emotion allows will. The will is all about making decisions. Humanity acts upon whatever the will decides.

In Christianity, a believer focuses on the will of God. What is God's will? Many of us say that phrase without really understanding its meaning. God's will is His decision for our lives. Now, what is God's decision for our lives? Our creator made everything good, and He made humanity in His own image (Genesis 1:27 NIV). God wants us to follow His way, His scripture, and His Holy Spirit. God's will is His decision to love and sacrifice Himself for all of humanity.

God told Abraham that He would make him fruitful and that a nation would come out of him (Genesis 17:6 NIV). God blessed Abraham greatly. That same blessing is available to everyone who believes in Jesus (Romans 10:9 NIV).

Thought and strong emotion, whether positive or negative, always result in a decision of the will. Men, women, and children are always making decisions. The best way to make a good decision is to examine our thoughts and emotions. Children need their parents to guide them in decision-making, as their parents are a vital resource of wisdom and knowledge. In that same way, we need God to guide our lives. The will is a daily decision to make a difference in our own lives, family, community, and world.

Body

God gave us our bodies, as He is their creator (Genesis 1:27 NIV). They are a gift and the temple of God (1 Corinthians 6:19, NIV). He resides in them. Whenever the idea or concept of Body is discussed, the issue of weight comes up. Most of us have a good reason for why we struggle with weight, and that is okay. The problem is not food but our soul. If we want to lose weight, we have to deal with our pain. Every struggle is caused by pain from our past. Most struggles or bad habits arise from hurt and emptiness.

To begin our healing and deliverance, we must write down every pain caused by parents, spouses, children, and others. Everyone has different hurts, but the healing process is the same. Once we determine the cause of the pain, we can find a solution and support system that will lead us to forgiveness.

Forgiveness will give us the freedom to work on our health and achieve victory in all aspects of our lives. Victory, in other words, is growth.

It is not just past mistakes but also the continuation of a wrong lifestyle that leads us away from victory. Our bodies are meant for the glory of God, which means everything should be done His way. In today's world, there are things being done with the body that displease God, such as drugs, rape, alcohol addiction, pornography, prostitution, pre-marital sex, and more. Are we willing to change, or will we continue to live in sin? God is always willing to forgive, but we must be willing to change. His love and mercy are available and waiting for us. Christianity is a faith that gives humanity a second chance at forgiveness and renewal by the power of the Holy Spirit. In other words, we must let go of the past and hang on to Jesus.

"You are to be holy to me because I, the LORD, AM HOLY, AND I HAVE SET YOU APART FROM THE NATIONS TO BE MY OWN" (Leviticus 20:26 NIV). Holiness transforms us into the image of God. In simpler terms, it involves taking care of ourselves in God's way. In whatever struggles we are facing, we must remember to deal with the root of the problem. The foundation is found in our thoughts and emotions. Examining our thoughts and emotions is crucial part of living a holy life.

Action

Action is the final product of soul. This behavior brings life and reality to our thoughts. It defines our faith in Christ and reflects how much we trust Him. Action is a judgment made by an individual to fix problems. Apostle Paul once said ". . . what I hate I do" (Romans 7:15 NIV) when talking about a sin. Everyone is faced with a decision that leads them to action. As Paul stated, we do what we don't want to do. A good action takes time and hard work, and consequently, it is natural to hate because people don't want to be patient. Wrong action is easy and instant; therefore, easy to love. The question is why.

Sin is a spirit that pressures us to act quickly. Swift action leads to hate, pain, crime, conflict, separation, and calamity. To resolve this, we must take a step back before making decisions. As we do, it is important to investigate situations. In society, investigations are done after a crime or wrong action is committed. Our actions are different, because they can be investigated beforehand. Action is the last step. Thought, emotion, and the will come first. We have opportunities every day to perform actions that positively impact our daily lives, and Christians have the Holy Spirit to remind and help them with examination and investigation.

"A hot-tempered person stirs up conflict, but the one who is patient calms a quarrel" (Proverbs 15:18 NIV). People who act quickly are hot-tempered. Their anger issues have a lot to do with hurt, neglect, rejection, and mistreatment as a child. If we have anger issues, it's important to deal with the hurt in our lives, as we are in danger. Hot-tempered persons are like people who think they can fly, which is impossible by nature. For a person to fly, he or she needs a machine. Conflict cannot be resolved with a hot-tempered person without patience and positive action. Patience is the hardest trait to develop, but it is also the most powerful weapon for a Christian. The Bible says, "Love is patient. . ." (1 Corinthians 13:4 NIV). When we are patient with ourselves and others, we show love. The minor soul maybe a follower of the major soul (thought) but it is essential in our life. When the minor soul is managed well, then our human nature will flourish.

CHAPTER THREE:
HUMAN NATURE

Human nature is a spirit given to us by our creator, God (Genesis 1:27 NIV). The gift of life—or spirit of life—was given to us after our nature was created (Genesis 2:7 NIV). Our nature came with a full package: the body, major soul (thought), and minor soul (emotion, will, action. The gift of life brought those components to life.

Before the fall of man, Adam and Eve were without sin. Their human nature was pure, as they had never eaten from the tree of the knowledge of good and evil (Genesis 2:16-17 NIV). They submitted to God and acted holy, righteous, and loving every day. Living for God's glory was as natural to them as eating, and they were good at it. Adam and Eve loved doing things God's way until they allowed sin into their thoughts.

We sin not because of a lack of Bibles, sermons, or worship songs but because we entertain the idea of sin. When our thought processes are defeated, they move into emotion, the will, action, and eventually sin. In Genesis 3, the serpent presents a question that tempts Eve's thought process. The act of responding without examination led Eve down the road of defeat. Human nature without God entertains the ways of the devil.

In Chapter One, I discussed the power of thought, which is the key to discovering our human nature. Human nature used to be pure but now it is contaminated by sin.

Human nature has basic needs that are gifts from God. These needs consist of:

1. God
2. Self-transformation
3. Family
4. Community
5. Calling and Career
6. Romance
7. Serving

These basic needs will always be part of humanity. Individuals can add more, but these ones will prepare people to live a life of joy and growth that is exciting and long-lasting.

Need for God

Every human needs God. Some accept the need, and others deny it. The latter will replace that need with atheism and other religions. Humanity has different belief systems because of varying experiences, such as hurts, failures, cultures, upbringings, and family backgrounds. These factors define and redefine the kind of faith we have. Google defines faith as a "complete trust or confidence in someone or something." Based on this definition, even atheists have faith, but their faith denies God and embraces reason and facts.

Atheists have faith in science and reason. As human beings, we cannot deny the DNA of God (Blessing and goodness) regardless of this evil world. The best way to understand our need for God is to recognize our need for parents. Parents provide wisdom, guidance, healthy development, and knowledge of God and His love. We need God like a child needs a father and mother.

Our need for God searches for one with a trustworthy word and Spirit. We all have insecurities—me, you, and even celebrities. Those insecurities turn into confidence when we turn to Jesus. Many might say they've heard that a thousand times, so what does that really look like?

I struggled with public speaking for years, and that made me insecure. My fear was a result of many factors. So, to deal with my fear of public speaking, I wrote down events from my life that caused me to be afraid. After making my list, I focused on solutions and ways I could practice. I began to participate in small groups, began to reject my fear, the act of forgiveness, and trust God.

Regardless of the factors, I needed to face my fears. To do so, I started to serve at my church and participate in a Bible study. I was hopeful. I admitted that I had a fear and that I would be okay if I faced it with God's help. It took a while, but I eventually grew comfortable with public speaking. I asked God to give me faith, endurance, and trust, and He provided. I'm not afraid to speak in public nowadays, because I know I am secure in God.

My success came when I sought God, became aware of the factors that caused my fears, admitted that I was afraid of public speaking, began to serve, and trusted God. Amidst this, the devil did everything he could to tempt, distract, and isolate me, but the word of God kept me strong, "The one who is in you is greater than the one who is in the world" (1 John 4:4, NIV). I needed God to help me deal with my fear of public speaking, and He was willing, but I had to be willing to show up and step forward.

When I was 11, my mom and I moved to Pasadena, California to live with my dad. I spoke zero English, because I hadn't learned it before coming to America. In Ethiopia, English is introduced to students when students get to Highschool. English was so hard that I gave up for many years. Writing and speaking in English were tough, and that frustrated me. I never thought I would survive my education.

During those years, I knew that I needed God, but I didn't know how to apply Him to my situation. I realize now that it was a miracle that I graduated from middle school, high school, and college. My accomplishment made me realize the beginning of my journey. God reminded me that I was loved and good things would happen if I did my part.

I remember crying out to God when I was young. School was hard, I had no friends, I couldn't speak English, I had so many enemies, and I wanted to go back to Ethiopia. In the midst of my pain, I turned to God. He understood me and helped me do my part. God was truly awesome, and He always will be.

Self-transformation

Self-transformation is one of the hardest things in life. Everyone on Earth is responsible for it. Its simple definition is: taking responsibility for wellbeing with consistent action. Human nature struggles with self-transformation, and that's why we have crime, racism, corrupt leadership, etc. Humanity avoids challenges and wants everything handed to them; however, there are those who play by the rules and make a positive impact on society. Life is full of challenges, and that's a problem for humanity. Most people ignore mistakes, failure, flaws, and hurts, but ignoring them does not make them disappear—in fact, they will be there until we die.

What is the key to transformation? Accepting our responsibility and acting upon on them. For example, if both married partners want to be right, and they refuse to comprise, then their relationship will be ruined. Why do people always have to be right? The answer is insecurity and low self-esteem. Insecurity and low self-esteem are a stumbling block for everything in life, and both men and women struggle with them. People hate themselves to the point of living in a wrong reality. Living a life without God, with no purpose, or savior is a wrong reality. Jesus gives solution to hate by stating, "Love the Lord your God with all your heart and with all your soul and with all your mind. This is the first and greatest commandment. And the second is like it: 'Love your neighbor as yourself" (Matthew 22:37–39 NIV).

Now let's talk about the second greatest commandment: to love our neighbor as ourselves. In order to love others, we must first love ourselves. Loving ourselves means being responsible for our action and always running toward God. We usually hate something about ourselves, such as our looks or attitude, and we tend to lash out at our loved ones because of it.

So, what is the solution? We must accept our aversion and change our perspective. If we step back and think about our mistakes, there is a good chance we can get back on track.

Christians tend to be grace-focused or truth-focused, but not both. Without grace and truth, there is no Christianity. Grace-focused people put little or no effort into improving their lives, and they trust God without the necessary effort. Truth-focused people try to improve their lives, but they put little effort into trusting God. People need grace and truth; otherwise, they will live in half-truth. The point is not to point fingers but to understand both sides. God always has a solution and way out for all circumstances. Jesus became a solution when He gave up His life to save all of humanity and provided eternal life.

When I first came to America, I was excited, shy, and unable to speak English. My world turned upside down when I went to elementary school a few months later, and it was a nightmare. I was bullied every day, and I always got in a fight. As a result, I became depressed, gained seventy pounds, and hated my life. It was then that I learned about my need for grace and truth.

After seven months of bullying, it became too hard for me to go to school. I needed to change schools. When the school year was over, I moved to a Christian middle school that changed my life. If not for Judson International school, I don't know if I would have survived high school. The school taught me English and about God and gave me hope and confidence. They cared, counseled, mentored, and prepared me to be a leader. I will always be grateful for them. Middle school was the best part of my life, because I gained confidence academically and in the knowledge that I was a child of God.

When I look back at elementary and middle school, I realize how much grace and truth God showed me. Everyone's situation may be different, but God's ability to make our situations better never changes. Dealing with bullies for seven months as a 12-year-old was not easy, and I sometimes wonder if I had stronger faith as a child. I hated the bullying, but I knew I needed to deal with it before I moved on. I asked God to help me then, which was my way of asking for a solution and His grace and favor. God came to my rescue, and I changed schools. He provided financially as well. As a child, I know God was proud of me for coming to Him for a solution.

Every child desires to walk and run, but it is hard to assume they will on the day they're born. But, with time and proper care, the child will walk. In the same way, we can transform our lives if we trust God and take that first step. Let us ask God to help us move forward in our lives.

Parent, Family, Relative

Parents can ruin or create a bright future for their kids. Childhelp. org states that "Every year more than 3.6 million referrals are made to child protection agencies involving more than 6.6 million children (a referral can include multiple children). The United States has one of the worst records among industrialized nations—losing on average between four and seven children every day to child abuse and neglect."

It is becoming normal for children to have single parents or no parents, which is dangerous, as it affects children, individuals, marriages, societies, and communities. Family separation is painful, and the result is devastating. The problem is not people but knowledge. ". . . my people are destroyed from lack of knowledge" (Hosea 4:6, NIV).

We have parents who aren't educated in parenting, and that is a red flag. Childhelp.org states that "Children who experience child abuse and neglect are about nine times more likely to become involved in criminal activity," which is scary and shows us how many parents are failing to take care of their children.

We don't teach young parents about parenting or young teenagers about sex, romance, dating, marriage, or family. If parents don't educate their children about the aforementioned topics, then society will. It is not easy, but when we decide to have kids, we sign up for the responsibility. As parents, we are responsible for teaching our kids about sex, romance, dating, marriage, and family. Many teenagers don't know what activities to be involved in or how to properly socialize or determine right from wrong. We need parents to make time for their children. Quality time is vital for them such as going out for coffee, lunch or dinner, go shopping, play sports, watch movies, hiking, or anything the child might like to do.

People in Ethiopia, America, and around the world can make a difference by being responsible. Presidents and prime ministers around the world should examine and strengthen family stability in their nations. A country's strength comes from sturdy and knowledgeable families.

Most people are thankful to have relatives as a support system. The beauty of relatives is that there is a strong, healthy boundary, just like siblings, that makes the relationship safe. In any relationship, including marriage, there are boundaries. Boundaries define a relationship and give it purpose. The most important aspects of a relationship with relatives are designated boundaries and Christ as the foundation. Boundaries provide safety, respect, etc. Relationship with a relative is a privilege and a gift. In the world we live in, people have ruined the concept of relationships with relatives. They are worthwhile when there are boundaries, Christ is at the center, and people respect and honor each other. God sets many boundaries so that we can enjoy life and live it in a righteous and holy manner.

Community

The simplest Google definition of community is a feeling of fellowship with others, as a result of sharing common attitudes, interests, and goals. It is crucial because it allows individuals to be part something greater than themselves, community. It is a place where people feel like they belong, are appreciated, and can grow. It is human nature to belong. As I grew older,

I appreciated my church community more. Fellowshipping with the body of Christ and striving toward Christ together are beautiful parts of the journey. Godly brotherhood and sisterhood is built in a church. I chose a community that put Christ as their foundation, because I valued that most. If we are honest with ourselves, being in a community is essential for life and our faith in God.

People research and ask to be part of a community. That is a great step, but we need to determine our values first. Values make life meaningful, give us a purpose for our existence and relationships, and determine how we live our lives, raise our children, and resolve problems. They are our foundation in life. Knowing our values will lead us to a community that fits our lifestyle. Unity based on truth drives a community toward dignity, innovation, and a secure future. Unity is good for the soul.

Calling and Career

Everybody has gifts, skills, and talents. We discover our potential in everyday life and at school. The concept of leadership evolves from the responsibility of daily life. Leadership has nothing to do with age, gender, titles position, or talents. It is defined by our responsibility with what is assigned to us. We can all be a leader if we're responsible.

To be effective with responsibility, we need to discover our passions and desires. People usually discover their calling in two ways: asking what they like to do and how they can make a difference in the world or by volunteering or finding a job.

Dating, Romance, Marriage

Marriage is a blessing from God. As I mentioned earlier, the younger generation needs to be educated about sex, romance, dating, and marriage. Adults need to educate themselves in these topics so that they can pass down godly wisdom and knowledge to their kids. At times, it is hard for a married adult to admit that they need to continue educating themselves about relationships, but marriage means going into the first grade, not graduate school. Romance in marriage is a lifelong experience.

To have a healthy church, strong families, and a great nation, we need healthy growing marriages. People want a happy and joyful life, but it requires hard work and continuous growth in knowledge and wisdom. In marriage, the greatest solutions are selflessness, understanding, and trust in God.

Serving

Serving involves helping others and expanding God's kingdom. People have different reasons for serving—some do it for an internship or career while others do it to help their church or give back to the community. Having a reason to serve makes serving meaningful, in the same way, we eat because we are hungry or we enjoy the food. However, regardless of our reason to serve, it's all about Jesus at the end of the day. Whether we are Christians or non-Christians, serving is all about being a light to the world, and that light is Jesus Christ, who sacrificed Himself so we can experience His love, grace, mercy, and eternal peace.

CHAPTER FOUR:
THE HOLY SPIRIT

The Spirit of God, which is God Himself in the spirit, is important for Christians to understand. The most powerful and underestimated spirit is the Holy Spirit. Numbers 11:24-25 says:

> "So Moses went out and told the people what the LORD had said. He brought together seventy of their elders and had them stand around the tent. Then the LORD came down in the cloud and spoke with him, and he took some of the power of the Spirit that was on him and put it on the seventy elders. When the Spirit rested on them, they prophesied—but did not do so again" (NIV).

Humanity had limited access to the Holy Spirit because of its sin. To fix this, Jesus died, taking the sins of the world and the wrath of God upon himself before resurrecting to victory. The elders, who experienced the Holy Spirit with Moses, had stay around the tent. For a little while, the spirit rested on them, and they prophesied. Their prophecies could have been about the future, the greatness of God, a vision, inner joy, wisdom of God, knowledge of God, love of God, the mercy of God, the grace of God, and the peace of God. Even though the availability to humanity was limited, God's power, strength, and love were still unlimited.

The soul needs a spirit to rely on, that is not human nature or the devil's spirit. The Spirit of God is the best spirit for the soul. Humanity needs a higher spirit to guide them, protect them, love them, and give them a purpose in life. The greatest hope for humanity is the Holy Spirit. Moses, the man of God who led the Israelites out of Egypt, always turned to God for help. He was an excellent example for every Christian. Going to God for His spirit is the wisest decision anyone can make.

The Spirit of God came upon people in the Old Testament, but He did not live in them. "The Spirit of God came on Azariah son of Oded" (2 Chronicles 15:1 NIV). Life must have been tough until the greatest hope arrived (John 1:14).

The Spirit of God is difficult to understand. I heard a lot about the Spirit of God as a kid, but I didn't really understand who He was. I made many mistakes because I was never taught about the Holy Spirit. As a teenager, I understood that I needed to read the Bible and do the right thing, but I had no idea that I could have a relationship with the Holy Spirit. It would have been so helpful to know that, as many years of loneliness could have been prevented. Many Christians live in sin and give up on life, God, community, and family because they do not know the Holy Spirit.

"Who is this King of glory? The LORD strong and mighty, the LORD mighty in battle" (Psalm 24:8 NIV). The Holy Spirit is full of glory, strength, and might. He is one with Jesus and God the father. So, why are many Christians confused about the Holy Spirit? Because they do not have a relationship with Him. Many pastors and preachers talk about relationship with God and Jesus, but they neglect the Holy Spirit. God the father, God the son (Jesus), and God the Holy Spirit play important roles in the lives of Christians. They are one God with different roles. Jesus said, "But the Advocate, the Holy Spirit, whom the Father will send in my name, will teach you all things and will remind you of everything I have said to you. Peace I leave with you; my peace I give you. I do not give to you as the world gives. Do not let your hearts be troubled and do not be afraid" (John 14:26-27 NIV).

When Jesus went to heaven, He sat on the right hand of God (Romans 8:34 NIV), leaving the advocator, the Holy Spirit, behind. That does not mean that Jesus and God are not with us—they are always with us. However, to unlock the ways of God and Jesus, we must have a relationship with Holy-Spirit. For Christians, the Holy Spirit must be in the picture. Jesus and God the Father, equally God, are also in the Holy Spirit.

The Holy Spirit is a spirit of God that can be discovered in every aspect of our lives. Some might argue that they can't hear an audible voice so they cannot have a conversation with the Holy Spirit, while others confuse Him with reasoning and logic.

I discovered the Holy Spirit because of a revelation from God. That revelation was having a relationship with the Holy-Spirit. For many years, I read the Bible but never felt the Holy Spirit. I know many Christians that still feel this way. It is frustrating to go through. Because I did not know the Holy Spirit, I gave God and Christianity a bad name, because I was not living a victorious life. My life changed when I discovered the greatest gift of all Jesus, who set me from all my sin and fear.

Word of God and the Holy Spirit

When we pick a book to read, we usually find one we like or relate to. For example, I do not particularly enjoy reading math books, as math is neither my area of interest nor my area of expertise. As a humanity major in college, I liked reading books on family, sociology, and psychology. Those subjects were easy for me to understand and apply in my life. Reading the Bible is like finding a book we like to read, except that the message is from God.

When we read school books, we begin with reason and research. When we read the Bible, we cannot use the same methods of logic and analysis, because the book doesn't start that way. Some people might jump to conclusions, saying they can't reason or research the Bible, but you can. It's how we start reading the Bible that's different.

The Bible is all about belief and trust. As Christians, we have to develop a complete trust in God's word and put our faith in Him. Many theologians reason and research instead of believing and trusting. Our understanding of the word of God, the Bible, will determine if we discover or miss out on the Holy Spirit.

When we read regular books, we learn about the thoughts, wisdom, knowledge, and life experiences of an imperfect author. On the other hand, God is the author of the Bible, and He is perfect and sinless (2 Corinthians 5:21 NIV). The Holy Spirit is also perfect and sinless. The Bible is the perfect thought, emotion, will, action, and word of God (Psalm 18:30 NIV).

The word of God is a voice from heaven that the Holy Spirit releases in our lives. In order to activate the Holy Spirit, the voice of God requires us to believe and trust. When we first accept Jesus into our hearts, we believe and trust, activating the

Holy Spirit. Many of us have deactivated the Holy Spirit and now live defeated lives.

If a person wants to have a Facebook, he needs the internet, friends, and an active account. Understanding the Bible is similar. It's about putting different elements together to activate the power, love, and grace of God in our lives.

Proverbs 3:5 says, "Trust in the Lord with all your heart and lean not on your own understanding" (NIV). What does this verse mean, and who is saying it? The speaker is one God, who is three, and the verse is a command from God, loving advice from Jesus, and comforting hope from the Holy Spirit.

We often think about Bible verses as quotes or essential phrases, but that is the wrong way to look at them. Our creator God, savior Jesus, and leader Holy Spirit wrote the Bible to communicate and build a relationship with us here on Earth. People don't take advice from strangers, they take it from people they love, respect, honor, and trust. The Holy Spirit, who reveals the work of God and Christ, is someone we love, respect, honor, and trust. The Bible makes sense and provides encouraging hope when we include the Holy Spirit in our faith walk.

Prayer and the Holy Spirit

Prayer is a conversation with God. For Christians to access the power of prayer, they must submit to the Holy Spirit. Obedience is one of the most significant ways to unlock the power of the Holy Spirit in prayer. Many people know the Bible, but they don't live it out through obedience. Prayer becomes powerful and effective when obedience is a part of daily life. Knowledge means nothing without action, just as prayer is nothing without obedience.

People want a bright future, so they read and research how

to have successful lives. The problem is not desire or knowledge. Most people lack action, therefore their knowledge and desire mean nothing. In Christianity, people want to discover the Holy Spirit, which is a start. However, they spend too much time only reading the Bible and spiritual books. They lack obedience to God's word, so they never discover the Holy Spirit.

Some individuals try to obey, but they give up if they don't see immediate results. Prayer is always connected with results, and that is a huge problem. A conversation with God should be focused on the relationship first. The relationship is focused on love, grace, mercy, boundaries, and obedience. Many people like that God is loving (1 John 4:8 NIV), graceful (John 1:14 NIV), and merciful (Luke 6:36 NIV), but they dislike His boundaries and desire for obedience (1 Samuel 15:22 NIV).

Sin is the biggest stumbling block in our prayer lives. When people pray, they usually focus on wants and needs and ignore their sin. This is a selfish prayer life. If we can't be real with the Holy Spirit, then we won't receive His assistance. As believers, we need the Holy Spirit in order to be true Christians; otherwise, we're just religious. Religion is all about following rules and never about having a relationship with God through the Holy Spirit. We need to be honest with the Holy Spirit so that we can have a relationship with God. If we reveal everything to God, then the Holy-Spirit can guide us.

"Rejoice always, pray continually, give thanks in all circumstances; for this is God's will for you in Christ Jesus" (1 Thessalonians 5:16-18 NIV). Rejoicing is being okay with living our lives according to God's ways. It's hard to understand the ways of God, because He thinks from an eternal perspective. Humans think from selfish and limited knowledge, which is why we clash with God. Whenever we disagree with Him, we say that we don't trust Him. We may have a good reason to question, but that does not mean we are right. Prayer groups are the least attended group in churches, because people are not okay with the way God does things. We cannot have a good prayer life unless we rejoice in God's ways. Rejoicing is directly related to obedience. The first step to a meaningful prayer life is to trust in the Lord, especially His word (Proverbs 3:5).

Once we trust God and are okay with His ways, we can begin our prayer journey. When it comes to prayer, people have many excuses, which reveals how much they disagree with God. Business is one of the most common reasons for why people don't pray. The Bible says to pray continually (1 Thessalonians 5:17 NIV), which means we can pray anytime, anywhere, and in any situation. We have time to eat, think, relax, and so on every day. During those times, we can talk to God about anything, but people always find a way to distance themselves from Him because they don't want to deal with the truth and their sin. Thus, they spend their whole lives running away from God.

When we have a runny nose, we have no problem cleaning it; however, when we have a destructive sin in our life and God tries to help us, we get offended to the point of hating and avoiding Him. We take what God says the wrong way and blame Him, because we don't want to deal with the truth. The truth is the sin, mistakes, weakness, and failures in our life. But, at the end of the day, we have to talk to God. He does not want to point out our failures. He wants to show us love. In that love, there is hope, freedom, strength, truth, humility, light, and meaningful relationship with God.

I pray that we would stop feeling insecure around God and let Him into our prayer lives. When it's dark, we turn on a light. In that same way, if we want God, Jesus, and the Holy

Spirit to be part of our lives, then we must obey, trust, and submit to God. To turn on the light, we must obey, submit, and trust.

Worship and the Holy Spirit

"God is spirit, and his worshipers must worship in the Spirit and in truth" (John 4:24 NIV). The most basic understanding of worship is singing Christians songs or songs that talk about God, Jesus, and the Holy Spirit. Worship is losing its meaning in today's Christianity. Its focus is on Christian traditions, feeling good emotionally, the musical instruments, and what songs to sing.

God being a spirit refers to the oneness that He has with Jesus and the Holy Spirit. Whether we worship alone or on Sunday morning, we must understand God's oneness. Believing in the oneness of God is the truth of God that is written in His word, "believe me when I say that I am in the Father and the Father is in me" (John 14:11 NIV). The Trinity has perfect union in spirit, which is important for the worshipper to believe and know. Doing so is the first step to understanding worship.

God's word emphasizes that we must have the Holy Spirit in our lives, which is the second step to understanding worship. God provided a savior for us in Jesus. When we accept Jesus, we receive the Holy Spirit, but Christianity doesn't stop there. Once we receive the Holy Spirit, we have to activate it by recognizing our need for God and living a life of repentance and obedience. Many people struggle to activate the Holy Spirit because they only repent or they only obey, but we must do both. Others don't obey or repent at all.

Why is repentance essential to worship? Because all have sinned and fallen short of the glory of God (Romans 3:23 NIV). Repentance is a desire and commitment to turn away from sin and follow God. To do this, we need supernatural support. "For it is by grace you have been saved, through faith—and this is not from yourselves, it is the gift of God—not by works, so that no one can boast" (Ephesians 2:8-9 NIV). Grace is our supernatural support. It is a free gift from God, and it is Jesus Christ, who died on the cross for our sins. We cannot be saved by our own works but by freely receiving grace. It is so powerful that it changes our lives forever.

Some people misuse grace and continue to live in sin. These people do not understand grace, as it leads to obedience. Anyone focused on grace but not obedience is confused and missing the point. True grace leads to obedience, while false understandings of grace trap us in sin.

Obedience is just as important as repentance when activating the Holy Spirit. It is simply doing what God says, an expression through action. Every person needs two legs to walk. A person with working legs has to stand up and take a step, otherwise he or she can't walk. The Holy Spirit is like a healthy leg. If we don't repent and obey, we won't be able walk. Many people have the Holy Spirit, but they have not activated Him. When we actively walk in our faith, our understanding of worship matures and grows. I pray that God will lead us to a lifestyle of repentance and obedience so that we can be worshippers.

The third step to understanding worship is truth. People can never know or understand the truth without obeying it. Truth is the written word of God, and the result of continued obedience is called transformation. Knowing the truth and being transformed by it are different. God does not want us to just know the truth; he wants us to be transformed by it. That is worship.

A life of obedience knows the truth. It's not about being perfect but always growing in reliance of God's grace. Today's society is full of information, but there's minimal transformation. We need to develop families, marriages, and societies that seek to obey God's truth. When we worship God, it is vital that we desire truth and transformation. Transformation and truth will strengthen our walk with God; otherwise, we may end up living a defeated faith.

When we go to work, our minds are on making money to provide. When we play professional sports, our minds are on winning. When we are married, our minds are on being a family and having a happy life. When we worship God, our minds should be on the first step (God being a spirit and His oneness with Jesus and the Holy Spirit), the second step (repentance and obedience), and the third step (truth and transformation). The next time we listen to worship songs in the car, on Sunday morning, or during devotion time, we should think about the answers that God provided us in John 4:24. In life, our driving force cannot be selfishness or human nature. It must be God, who is our creator, redeemer, protector, guide, and father.

Relationship and the Holy Spirit

The Holy Spirit will intervene in every area of our lives, including our relationships. Whether we are single for five years or married for fifty, the Holy Spirit will be involved if we allow Him to be. Every relationship must focus on God and be led by the Holy Spirit. In today's world, people have messed up relationships, marriages, and families, and the dysfunction ruins every aspect of their lives. Everyone has a sinful past, but society embraces it. The cycle of a dysfunctional past is destroying our nation. Divorce and family separation are becoming the norm. The Holy Spirit is the only hope and solution for relationships. I discovered the Holy Spirit later on in my life, and I sometimes wish I had found God's spirit sooner, because it would have saved me from many evil choices.

Relationships have no meaning today. Humanity breaks every rule, because it doesn't have the Holy Spirit. First graders are dating, and people think it's cute, but it's dangerous. At those ages, kids and teenagers should focus on building relationships with their family and friends. Kids dating and having children early on are a result of irresponsible and neglectful parents who put their job and career before their family. When we have parents who avoid blessings and responsibilities, the Holy Spirit can't intervene in their lives or the lives of their children. Their children will be adults one day, and they will make the same mistakes as their parents. Dysfunctional behavior and decisions are passed down from generation to generation.

We need the Holy Spirit, as it gives us purpose in our relationships. God wants us to be mature before we date. Maturity helps us deal with hurt, diversity, miscommunication, and misunderstanding. It is God's way of protecting our marriages and our children's marriages. When parents spend quality time with their children and put energy into raising them, kids don't run around seeking love and attention. If parents don't have the Holy Spirit, then it becomes harder for children to have it. When it comes to relationships and the Holy Spirit, parenting will always be a part of the conversation. Everyone has been a child with a legal or biological parent. The only people who did not were the first people, Adam and Eve.

After we reach a mature age, God wants us to be spiritually stable. Stability focuses on our relationship with God and our moral compass. The Holy Spirit wants our moral compass to be healthy and growing. If parents don't teach morals at home, then the next generation will create ones that are not focused on God. Dating, relationships, and marriage require morals focused on God and His word. Doing the right thing in a relationship is not a one-time thing, it's a lifestyle. We don't have to understand God to be a Christian. We just need to trust Him. Relationships are built on trust.

"Wait for the Lord; be strong and take heart and wait for the Lord" (Psalm 27:14 NIV). The Holy Spirit loves patience, especially while we wait on God. When individuals are patient, then they can see the full picture of God in their life. It's important to be patient in a relationship. Patient in a relationship allows us to be in somebody else's shoes so that we can show them empathy. Waiting focuses on righteousness, holiness, obedience, and God's will. Patience is godly, and it requires practice and discipline.

Being impatient is like a contagious disease, and it can have a major impact on our relationships. When parents are impatient, it's likely that their children will be as well. When teachers and business leaders are impatient, their students and customers are in danger. Lack of patient in business and teaching hinders growth and learning.

The best way to be patient is to examine and wait. "Examine yourselves to see whether you are in the faith; test yourselves. Do you not realize that Christ Jesus is in you—unless, of course, you fail the test?" (2 Corinthians 13:5 NIV). Examination and waiting resolve impatience. God encourages and commands patience for productive relationships. The Holy Spirit wants us to be patient with one another, because people are imperfect. Marriage is two imperfect people trying to grow and live a happy life. The maturation process requires us to be patient with one another.

Godliness is directly connected to patience. A lifestyle of godliness involves hoping in Christ and knowing the Holy Spirt will provide the solutions we need. In today's world, we have everything right in front of us, so nothing challenges us to be patient. Most people have been impatient, but when they enter a relationship, they're shocked by their impatience. Patience is not fun or exciting, but it is rewarding. We're rewarded when our marriage and work place grow and our children head in the right direction.

People are willing to have great relationships, but they are not willing to be patient. A relationship will never work if we are not willing to be patient. Our children, employees, and people in general need our patience, and whether we like it or not, the Holy Spirit asks us to be. Life always gives us situations and opportunities for patience. We cannot escape it, so we need to embrace it and obey the Holy Spirit.

Communication is the biggest stumbling block in relationships, and it sometimes leads to misunderstandings and divorce. Many Christians don't think about the Holy Spirit when it comes to communication. The norm is to run to a pastor or marriage counselor for every problem. Counseling is important, but running to God should always be our first step. Most marriages can survive and grow if we run to God. When we communicate with our partner, we need the Holy Spirit to intervene; thus, problems arise when one or neither spouse has the Holy Spirit. However, just because we've received the Holy Spirit does not mean we allow Him to work in our lives, just like having a treadmill in our home does not make us active people. To be active, we have to use the treadmill. In that same way, we must surrender to the Holy Spirit so that He can be active in our lives. Surrender is giving up our way so that God can be glorified and in charge. When two people have the Holy Spirit, their communication is godly and effective. Many issues arise in relationships, but if we have God, we will be okay.

Christianity requires us to have the Holy Spirit. As children of God, we always need to seek Him and His spirit. "Come near to God, and he will come near to you" (James 4:8 NIV).

The Holy Spirit and Leadership

"The Spirit of the Lord came on him, so that he became Israel's judge and went to war. The Lord gave Cushan-Rishathaim king of Aram into the hands of Othniel, who overpowered him. So the land had peace for forty years, until Othniel son of Kenaz died" (Judges 3:10-11 NIV).

In the world we live in, leadership is about work experience and rising to the top. However, we see in Judges that it's not about that in God's eyes. Leadership is about having His Spirit as the foundation. The Israelites needed a leader, and God provided one who had His Spirit. As a result, the nation of Israel had peace for 40 years. Relationships, families, communities, societies, and the world suffer because we do not have leaders with the Holy Spirit. The Holy Spirit sees the bigger picture. He is the foundation of knowledge and the beginning of wisdom. The all-knowing, eternal God.

Why do leaders fail in their leadership? One reason is that their focus and mindset are self-centered. These kinds of leaders have insecurities and many failures. All they think about is success and saving the world. They are more interested in being a savior than a child of God, but God never asked us to be saviors. He asked us to rely on Him when we face obstacles. Leaders who think they can save the world are leaders who do not have the Holy Spirit. Selfish mindsets reflect childhood mistreatment, and those people strive to prove the world wrong. God can raise anyone to do His work, but those people are missing the point: It's not about us. It's about Jesus.

The second reason leaders fail is that they don't know how to prioritize. Many leaders get married and then abandon their wife or husband for success. It's dangerous to have too much of a good thing. Those individuals have a severe addiction that needs serious attention. Real success requires us to prioritize what's essential. A leader's first responsibility is his marriage. The number of educated leaders who can't even take care of their families is sickening. Many of them think the world needs them instead of Jesus, and, sadly, those leaders have children just to bring pain into the world. Abandoning one's family is becoming a norm in society. Why can't men and women see the pain they cause their spouse and kids? Why do they keep living as if they are not the problem? The answer is simple: the Holy Spirit is inactive in their lives. Their selfish human nature has taken over, causing them to fail as leaders.

The third reason leaders fail is that they are not team players. Many only care about their titles or number of degrees. As a youth pastor and supervisor, I learned that leadership is not about position or title but the ability to work with a team. Title-focused leaders get the job done without teambuilding, but teambuilding is more important than a completed job—though many leaders would disagree. Whether we work for an organization, church, government, or our own business, teambuilding is crucial. Many organizations fail because they assign tasks and projects before they do teambuilding. This is one of the biggest reasons that church plantings fail. In the Christian faith, a church can't become the body of Christ without teambuilding.

Leaders who are not team players need to take classes on teambuilding if they want to be effective leaders. Every position in the world requires that leaders have a strong team, as they are the backbone of good leadership. God, Jesus, and the Holy Spirit are the perfect example of teamwork.

The final reason that leaders fail is they have the wrong idea about their legacy. Many people spend their whole lives trying to be famous, but that's not what leaving a legacy is about. It's about the impact we have on others.

There are well-known, selfish sports players whose legacies have little impact on the game, and there are also team players who give meaning to the game. Athletes use their talents to make the game beautiful, not accomplish something. It's about the beauty of the game instead of individual talent. Leadership is not about the title but the beauty of teambuilding. Similarly, Christianity is not about us but the glory of God.

Leaders succeed because they learn from their mistakes, and they are selfless even while they take care of themselves. These leaders prepare the next generation for leadership. When leaders want to be glorified by others, they forget to think about the future. They leave the next generation in poverty while enjoying their success, but successful leaders make sure the next generation prospers. Developing successful leaders is just as important as being a good leader. We need holistic, impartial leaders who think about the present and the future.

Another reason that leaders succeed is that they are good at prioritizing. Effective leadership begins with home management. Home stability comes from a secure marriage and well-tended children. Leaders cannot trade home responsibility for work success and world change. Those who do are ineffective leaders who damage their organization more than they help. Whether we like it or not, our home life is vital to our work and the next generation. As leaders, we must understand that success starts at home and ends at work. Our relationships with our spouse and children say a lot about our leadership.

"Politically, economically, and socially, our nations are experiencing turmoil and moral decay—characterized by crime, religious conflict, economic uncertainty, the unequal distribution of resources, political corruption, civil unrest, the disintegration of family, cybercrime, poverty, disease, famine, sexual abuse, greed, racial clashes "cleansing," global terrorism, and war" (Munroe, 2014, p. 9).

Dr. Myles Munroe states many of the problems we face in the 21st century. The world is a mess, and we need leaders that can bring humanity out of it. Team-oriented leaders are the ones who will give us hope. We need to come together to fight this chaos. Humanity is at its best when it works together. Everyone is a leader, and we need to act like it. Everyone has a role to play, and each role is equally important. Leaders who value and empower others will change the world. The mess that exists in this world cannot be avoided, but it can be faced with courage. We need courageous leaders who create and build effective leadership in society. Success begins with leaders who are team players.

Our character will determine our legacy. In life, we must have something to fight for. I believe that we must fight for truth. Being truthful with ourselves and each other will give us a foundation, meaning, and purpose.

The greatest freedom is found in truth. "Then you will know the truth, and the truth will set you free" (John 8:32 NIV). The truth weakens the devil's attacks, reveals and activates the Holy Spirit, provides confidence and hope for the future, and allows us to make a difference. The truth is the foundation of Christianity and knowing the Holy Spirit. The truth is our savior, Jesus Christ. "Jesus answered, 'I am the way and the truth and the life. No one comes to the Father except through me'" (John 14:6 NIV).

Discovering the Holy Spirit in the Soul and Soul Organization

The Trinity, God being three in one, is hard for Christians to grasp. In the midst of the confusion, we need to discover the Holy Spirit. To find Him, we must understand and review the soul, which is discussed in the first two chapters. The major soul is thought, the minor soul is emotion, will, body, and action, and the influential spirits are human nature, the Holy Spirit, and Lucifer's Spirit. Everything that happens in our lives originates from the major soul. To discover the Holy Spirit, we have to understand the power of our thoughts. "The tongue has the power of life and death, and those who love it will eat its fruit" (Proverbs 18:21 NIV). What comes out of our mouths originates in our conscious and unconscious thoughts. We discover the Holy Spirit in our thought process. Humanity's thoughts are full of junk and wickedness, so it's hard to understand the Holy Spirit amidst a sinful lifestyle. However, we are not trying to be perfect either. No matter what we do, if we confess our sins, we will be forgiven.

A good example is a parent-child relationship. Most parents don't want their children to disobey them. It hurts and saddens parents when their children misbehave instead of seek their help. The Holy Spirit is like our parent, and He wants us to ask for His help. During our time on Earth, He is our guide and helper, while still being one with Jesus and God the father. For example, in marriage, God gave men a spiritual leadership role, but men are one with their wives, making women spiritual leaders as well. So, who is the leader in marriage? Both the husband and the wife.

The Holy Spirit lives in us and guides our lives in a similar manner, meaning that we are simultaneously led by God, Jesus, and the Holy Spirit. True parenting happens when a husband and wife work together as a couple instead of as individuals. Humanity's parents are God, Jesus, and the Holy Spirit, who work in perfect unity to guide and protect us. When God created the heavens and the earth, He was not the only one. Jesus and the Holy Spirit were equally part of creation. When Jesus suffered and died on the cross, God and the Holy Spirit suffered as well.

Now that we know that God, Jesus, and the Holy Spirit take different roles but participate equally, we can discover the Holy Spirit in our thoughts and lives. On Earth, the purpose of the Holy Spirit is to lead the soul, and God and Jesus equally participate. The soul consists of thought, emotion, will, body, and action, and the Holy Spirit wants to help us manage it all. Within the Soul Organization, the CEO (the Holy Spirit) and His equal participants (God and Jesus) are in charge of the manager (thought). The manager is in charge of the employees (emotion, will, body, and action). The owner of the Soul Organization is God, Jesus, and the Holy Spirit.

"Do you not know that your bodies are temples of the Holy Spirit, who is in you, whom you have received from God? You are not your own; you were bought at a price. Therefore honor God with your bodies" (1 Corinthians 6:19-20 NIV). In this verse, "bodies" and "temples" refer to the soul. When it says you are not your own, God is claiming ownership of the Soul Organization, which means He is the creator of the soul.

The Soul Organization's biggest problem lies with the manager (thought). It wants to be the CEO (God, Jesus, and the Holy Spirit), thereby corrupting the organization. The manager is responsible for this. "The LORD saw how great the wickedness of the human race had become on the earth, and that every inclination of the thoughts of the human heart was only evil all the time" (Genesis 6:5 NIV). In other words, God saw that the manager had become more wicked. The manager has fought the CEO for generations, because it focuses on power and hates the owner and its assigned position. The manager's inability to accept the position, because of pride and insecurity, leads to conflict. It does not trust the CEO.

In the Old Testament, the CEO (the Holy Spirit) had a hard time playing His role because the manager (thought) would not listen or allow Him to lead the Soul Organization (Genesis 6:5 NIV). Because of the manager, the CEO visited people rather than residing in them. Because of the manager's selfish choice, many generations have missed out on the CEO's leadership. The Soul Organization has been corrupted to the point of destruction.

Thus, the CEO gathered for a meeting focused on building trust. They were concerned because the Soul Organization was in chaos. To rebuild trust and help the manager (thought), Jesus came to Earth in human form, suffered for humanity's failures, wickedness, and sin, took on the wrath of God, and then resurrected three days later. Jesus did this, but God and the Holy Spirit participated in it.

This was the best way to help people trust in God, as trust leads to belief and salvation. Now that the process of building trust had begun, humanity needed to return to the Holy Spirit for guidance and leadership. Jesus's greatest act was to build trust so that we would know Him. The manager was supposed to change its leadership and the way it functioned; however, even after the CEO's sacrifice, the manager remained wicked and doubtful.

"Trust in the LORD with all your heart and lean not on your own understanding; in all your ways submit to him, and he will make your paths straight" (Proverbs 3:5-6 NIV). This verse concerns the manager, as the manager relies on its own ways and not the Holy Spirit's leadership. It is a command that is vital for the manager and the soul. Jesus has done everything in His power, so that we would allow the Holy Spirit to lead and guide us. I pray that we all allow the Holy Spirit to do His part before we come to our own ruin. The manager must submit to the Holy Spirit; otherwise, the Soul Organization and its employees (emotion, will, body, and action) will suffer and be destroyed.

The soul's responsibility is an individual's highest priority. The responsibility is to rely on God, take good care of self, and glorify God. The Soul Organization can go two ways: if there is trust, then the soul will deal with conflict, and if there is not, then the soul will be defensive and turmoil will ensue.

"All great relationships, the ones that last over time, require productive conflict in order to grow. This is true in marriage, parenthood, friendship, and certainly business" (Lencioni, 2002, p.202). The foundation of our soul is the manager (thought). The manager avoids conflict when it does not trust the Holy Spirit, resulting in a life with many problems. Christianity is heading towards conflict, because believers are trusting God, Jesus, and the Holy Spirit less. Whether we like it or not, the soul will experience conflict and suffering in this life.

The manager (thought) creates all of the conflict because it is selfish and ignores the CEO (the Holy Spirit). Funnily enough, the manager thinks about the wrong things and is therefore defeated by its own desires. Thoughts lead to false emotion, will, and action without the Holy Spirit's management, and conflict continues while we mistrust Him.

The soul hates submitting to a higher power, especially the Holy Spirit, and it does not get along with others. The soul deals with day-to-day functions, so many families, marriages, relationships, organizations, and societies that are in chaos because people refused to deal with the Soul Organization.

We live in a society that avoids dealing with conflict at all times; thus, we should not be surprised when children, families, leaders, and organizations are a mess. Patrick Lencioni talks about the five dysfunctions of a team in a business organization, and they include trust and conflict. I, on the other hand, am talking about the Soul Organization that makes us who we are as individuals.

The biggest similarity I see between Ethiopia and America is that avoiding conflict is the norm, and this concerns me about my well-being. Avoiding conflict never has a good outcome or ending. God gives humanity the choice to be in charge or submit to His Spirit, and the manager (thought) will always choose to be in charge unless it submits to the CEO (God, Jesus, and the Holy Spirit).

To solve the problem of not dealing with conflict, we must trust God and realize that the Holy Spirit is the solution. The soul, just like an organization, has to deal with conflict; otherwise, it will be in trouble. Every avoided conflict will lead to dysfunction. The manager has to be a leader willing to deal with conflict right away. In the soul, the manager (thought) has to be able to deal with conflict that occurs in the thought process.

Once conflict leaves the thought process, it descends through emotion, will, body, and action to become a lifestyle. If we notice conflict in our thought process, we must seek help, which depends on whether we trust our surrounding of the Holy-Spirit. Seeking help will always start with approaching the CEO (the Holy Spirit).

The Soul Organization has a protocol concerning the chain

of command and dealing with conflict. We have to respect and do what our CEO (the Holy Spirit) tells us to do. After going to our CEO, we need to confront the conflict we are facing. More often than not, people don't want to admit their struggle because of shame, so they keep quiet and make it worse. Facing our struggles may not be easy, but it will save our lives. Dealing with conflicts within an organization might not be a pleasant experience, but it helps the organization grow.

What we do with our lives and the decision we make is vital, and we are responsible for our Soul Organization. Dealing with conflict means doing things we do not like, just like some people hate exercising even though it's essential for their health. We desire a great life, but we do not want to do the hard work it takes to have one.

Finally, the Soul Organization needs to commit to God. Commitment means following the ways of God without wavering. Our morals and lifestyle have to imitate Jesus Christ. God is our creator, Jesus is our savior, and the Holy Spirit is our advocate and guide, yet they are one and participate equally in each other's roles.

Many struggle with commitment because they're missing two crucial steps. If each step is not followed, we cannot get to the commitment stage. To have a successful Soul Organization, the manager (thought) must build trust with the CEO (the Holy Spirit), deal with conflict with the Holy Spirit's help, and fully commit to God.

Commitment's last step happens as we accomplish steps one and two. The Soul Organization's employees (emotion, will, body, and action) are usually powerless, because they obey everything the manager (thought) says. Similarly, it is not easy to be a Christian led by the Holy Spirit, but it is worth it. The hardest jobs have the greatest rewards. Some Christians want to commit to God so that they can live a good life without any effort, which is disrespectful and utterly offensive to God. They want to trust God without trusting the Holy Spirit for guidance and dealing with the conflict in their lives. We respect and honor Him when we commit to working hard in our personal and professional lives.

Society talks about many institutions—marriage, family, business, government, cults, etc.—but not the soul. Soul development is important to God, because we are created in His image. God is the designer of the soul; therefore, humanity must understand the manufacturer's purpose. Soul Organization focuses on our identity in Christ, which requires us to trust the Holy Spirit in every circumstance.

CHAPTER FIVE:
LUCIFER'S SPIRIT

The devil, Lucifer, is a misunderstood spirit that's destroying humanity. It is essential to know the truth about the devil. Humanity's identity failed and suffered because of sin. God is perfect in all his ways (Psalm 18:30 NIV), and the devil is evil in all his ways. He is the father of liars (John 8:44).

Let's look at the devil's abilities and knowledge to see how he operates. The devil has thought, emotion, and will, and the majority of humanity is unaware of it. Creator God has thought, emotion, and will as well. The difference between God and humans is that God's thought, emotion, and will are perfect. The devil's thought, emotion, and will are always wicked. God gets us out of a mess, while the devil puts us back in.

When the devil attacks, he always targets thought. The devil knows that humanity's greatest weapon is their thoughts and that he will win if he can control them. He's after humans because he's jealous that God would do anything for them. When the devil chose to become the father of liars, he rejected God's truth. The devil was once a child of God until he chose to be His enemy.

The power of thought is like the internet. The internet

contains useful knowledge and wisdom, in addition to wickedness that destroys lives, and it can be useful when used wisely. God's thought is a perfect internet—no wicked websites exists within it. The devil's thought is an evil internet filled with horrible websites. Even when the website seems decent, its purpose is to destroy humanity. Human thought, however, is like an internet filled with both good and bad websites, and our choices will determine our present and future.

The devil is looking for opportunities to ruin human lives, whether they are Christian or not. In order to resist the devil, we need to secure our lives in Christ every day. It's common for people to think that the devil attacks after we fall into sin, but that is ignorance. The inception of sin and our fall always begin with our thoughts, and unexamined thoughts give the devil the power to destroy us. Devil is coming after us, and we must prepare ourselves for battle. "Finally, be strong in the Lord and in his mighty power. Put on the full armor of God, so that you can take your stand against the devil's schemes" (Ephesians 6:10–11 NIV). We need God to guard our thoughts from the schemes of the devil on a daily basis. Unless our thoughts are walking toward righteousness, holiness, and truth, we are in danger being attacked by the devil. Without God, our thoughts are vulnerable to sin.

The devil doesn't attack our emotion and will that much, because they follow our thoughts; thus, we need to be aware of our thought process at all times. If we allow the enemy to take control of our thoughts, then we'll have a dysfunctional life until we die. We ruin our lives when we give in to the enemy.

Let's look at what the devil does once he controls our thoughts.

First, the devil does everything he can to make us distrust God. Trust is the foundation of our victory in God, Jesus, and the Holy Spirit. The devil doesn't want us to take that first step, so he will always put us in a position to distrust God. Trusting God means pushing away everything that is not from Him, including the devil. Being pushed away is the end of the devil; therefore, he retaliates. He wants us to create distrust between God, spouses, children, relatives, churches, businesses, and societies. Humanity's goal in life is to trust God and bring Him glory—the opposite of the devil's purpose. The devil will try as hard as he can to keep us from trusting God and bringing Him glory.

Trust is so powerful, yet we neglect it in our lives. The devil hates trust, but he hates actions that place trust in God more. To destroy our enemy, we must trust God. The devil exploits our weaknesses to ruin our lives, so we must attack his weaknesses. His greatest weakness is humanity living out their trust in God.

Second, the devil loves when we conflict with God. We cannot avoid conflict, because conflict is a way of life. It is an opportunity for us to grow. Most don't see the beauty of conflict, so they spend their whole lives avoiding it. The devil rejoices when conflicts are avoided, because he knows that the individual is heading toward self-destruction.

The devil wanted to be just like God, but that was impossible, so he chose to conflict with his creator. From the beginning, the devil built his foundation on conflict. Many people don't want to be Christians, because there is a lot of conflict in the Bible and the lives of believers. People get into crime, addiction, and other lousy lifestyles because of conflict in their lives. Churches split, marriages change from united to divorced, politicians say and do horrible things, and countries go to war because of conflict. We have a chaotic world, because the devil uses avoided conflict to be in control. When a problem occurs, humanity retaliates by adding more conflict, which gives the enemy more power. Society seeks peace without dealing with conflict, thereby falling into the devil's trap.

"My people are destroyed from lack of knowledge" (Hosea 4:6 NIV). Ignorance and lack of wisdom and understanding are destroying humanity. Schools, churches, and businesses need to teach the beauty of conflict. Facing conflict leads to growth, while avoiding conflict begins a miserable life. We have a choice to make: to face reality with the help of God or surrender to the devil. Now is the time to ask God to help us face our conflict. If we continue to avoid conflict, then we won't be committed to God.

Commitment is essential to security in God. The devil wants us to be committed to him instead. Our lives are led, affected, or transformed by the one we choose to follow and glorify. Committing to God is glorifying God. Committing to the devil is glorifying the devil, as is committing to ourselves.

Commitment is not just a saying but something that requires action and consistency. A dedicated person has hope, focuses on action, and sticks to the truth. The devil, on the other hand, destroys hopes, focuses on empty promises, and sticks to lies.

Many of us commit to our work because we get paid, but we don't commit to our personal lives. When it comes to life, people don't care how they function as long they stay alive. The way we live our lives is more significant than our weekly paycheck. The devil does not want us to know that committing to God is worth more than a billion dollars. It is our responsibility to seek the truth before the devil blinds us. It's a fact that committing to sports and school will steer us in the right direction but resisting the enemy by committing to God will give us even greater joy. "Rejoice in the Lord always. I will say it again: Rejoice!" (Philippians 4:4 NIV).

CHAPTER SIX:
UNDERSTANDING
SALVATION

Understanding salvation begins with knowing who our creator is and how much He knows about us.

> "For you created my inmost being; you knit me together in my mother's womb. I praise you because I am fearfully and wonderfully made; your works are wonderful, I know that full well. My frame was not hidden from you when I was made in the secret place, when I was woven together in the depths of the earth. Your eyes saw my unformed body; all the days ordained for me were written in your book before one of them came to be" (Psalm 139:13–16 NIV).

Nobody is a mistake. Before we were conceived in our mother's womb, God set a plan for each of us.

"According to the current estimates, the world population reached 7 billion in 2012 and the new projections indicate that the 8 billion marker will be reached in 2025. (The Census Bureau's International Data Base estimates that the world population will reach 7.5 billion on September 19, 2018 at 12:22 a.m. EDT)" (U.S. Census Bureau, 2018).

God wonderfully made every person in the world. It does not matter whether children are planned or unplanned, God has a purpose for all of humanity.

When we decide to invite Jesus into our hearts, we are saying and believing that God is our wonderful creator and He knows everything about us. Faith begins with trusting a God who knows humanity's beginning and ending. The fact that God is our creator provides us with great hope. We must take that hope and make it a part of our lives.

God knows everything; therefore, there is no reason to worry about the future. If people knew and believed that God was in control, then they would be less anxious. As a child and an adult, being wonderfully made was not a concept that I thought about. The moment I realized my creator created me, a significant weight lifted off my shoulders. People tend to be insecure and make the wrong decisions because they don't know how special they are. Being unique is knowing that there is a God who created us with fantastic knowledge, wisdom, and power. God is always present, and He will never leave us. Salvation gives us assurance that the creator is still watching over His creation.

"Now this is eternal life: that they know you, the only true God, and Jesus Christ, whom you have sent" (John 17:3 NIV). In African culture, if a parent knows his child and the child respects his parent, then that is an accomplished relationship. But everything is different with God. God knows his children and gives them the opportunity to know Him. In African culture, parents do not open up to their kids, because it is considered inappropriate. As a result, parents miss out on building strong bonds of trust with their children. God opens up to humanity in Genesis to Revelation, which means He wants to build a bond of trust with us. The most important thing to us is knowing God, because He already knows everything about us. The best way for parents to build a relationship with their child is to let them know about themselves, as this establishes trust.

It is hard to trust people we do not know. Once we know God, we will truly understand eternal life. Many people deny Christ because they don't know Him. Some Christians are so concerned about themselves that they never take a step toward recognizing their savior.

In Christianity, God wants a relationship with us so He can reveal truth and provide salvation. He wants to spend times with us. Quality times is vital for God to build relationship with us. In society, some fathers and mothers don't desire to spend time with their children; they don't value quality time. In Christianity, it's humanity who does not make time for God. Some Christians avoid God and make excuses for not spending quality time with Him. Whenever something goes wrong, we blame God, because we see our faults. Our faults reflect our anger and frustration at doing the wrong things. God makes no mistakes, because He is perfect at all times, and his desire for relationship is not temporary but eternal and everlasting.

"For God so loved the world that he gave his one and only Son, that whoever believes in him shall not perish but have eternal life" (John 3:16 NIV). God is a loving father who expresses His love with words and action. God gives us everything we ask and more. Expressed love becomes effective when we respond to it. To fully experience the power of God, we have to jump into the pool of God's grace, protection, and everlasting kindness. As Christians, we cannot stay on the edge and pretend to swim in the pool, as many in the church do. Churches continue to live in sin. They're closing and have low attendance because people do not jump into God's pool of grace, love, and mercy. Our creator took a risk when He placed His confidence in us, and we must do the same.

Luke 1:37 says, "For no word from God will ever fail" (NIV). In other words, God will never fail us despite humanity failing Him so many times. When we fail God, we assume it's okay and continue in our sinful lifestyle, and God continues to give us chances to return to Him. Salvation is experiencing the everlasting love of God on Earth and then in heaven when our time here is done.

"If anyone, then, knows the good they ought to do and doesn't do it, it is sin for them" (James 4:17 NIV). The good that we are called to do is in the Bible (Psalm 37:3 NIV). "Turn from evil and do good; seek peace and pursue it" (Psalm 34:14 NIV). God pours out His heart in the Bible so that we would do good.

We have a lot of information in this day and age. At school, when our teachers ask us to do an assignment, we give them a response. We say "yes," because we know how to do the assignment, and sometimes we say "no," because we are rebellious or damaged in our friendships and home life. At times, we respond "I can't," because we are unable to do an assignment. We give God similar answers. Saying "yes" to God brings us closer to Him. Saying "no" keeps us hopeless. Responding with "I can't" is like saying no, therefore we need to ask God for help. "I can do all this through him who gives me strength" (Philippians 4:13 NIV). God is our helper, and we need to trust Him.

"For all have sinned and fall short of the glory of God" (Romans 3:23 NIV). People interpret this verse two ways: as an excuse to live in sin or to deny their sinful nature in an attempt to be perfect. Hunger for self-glory destroys humanity's relationship with God. People will always fail God, which is why He provided us with a savior who is full of grace and mercy. We were created to bring God glory. Doing so will protect us and give us hope and strength to resist every temptation.

If we embrace sin, we will reap the seed that we sow. "For the wages of sin is death, but the gift of God is eternal life in Christ Jesus our Lord" (Romans 6:23 NIV). Sin—especially the outcome of sin—is dangerous, but people continue to embrace it. When we miss tests and assignments, we get bad grades. The individual is responsible for their bad grades. Sin is a self-destructive decision that damages people's souls. It is a cause-and-effect situation. The wrong action causes sin, and its outcome devastates the present and the future. "But your iniquities have separated you from your God; your sins have hidden his face from you" (Isaiah 59:2 NIV). Sin not only destroy us but also our relationship with God, just as a husband damages his relationship with his spouse if he continually hurts her.

"Jesus answered, 'I am the way and the truth and the life. No one comes to the Father except through me'" (John 14:6 NIV). Christianity begins with knowing the way, truth, and life of Jesus Christ. In the academic and scientific world, facts are crucial and highly valued. In the Christian faith, truth and belief with action based in the love, grace, mercy, and righteousness of God are essential. Children need parents, students need teachers, and humans need Jesus. A heart, leg, and eye are crucial for a body to function. The soul of a human and its parts (thought, emotion, will, body, and action) will not function without the truth of Jesus.

"For Christ also suffered once for sins, the righteous for the unrighteous, to bring you to God. He was put to death in the body but made alive in the Spirit" (1 Peter 3:18 NIV). Jesus took the blame to save us. He didn't have to die, but He did, because His love was greater than we can imagine. "But God demonstrates his own love for us in this: While we were still sinners, Christ died for us" (Romans 5:8 NIV). Jesus Christ is the only way we can get near to God. The most important day of our lives is the day we allow Jesus into our heart.

"If you declare with your mouth, 'Jesus is Lord,' and believe in your heart that God raised him from the dead, you will be saved" (Romans 10:9-10 NIV). This is not an easy verse to understand, but its meaning is powerful. "Jesus is Lord" is not just a saying. Any word that comes out of our mouths originates in our thoughts. When we read Romans 10: 9-10, it is crucial that we know how the verse processes in our soul. When people think about Jesus being Lord, they typically don't go through the whole process being saved. When people repeat God's word, it usually goes from their thought process to their emotion and stops at will (making a decision). It does not go to the action phase, which is necessary to activate the meaning of "Jesus is Lord." Some Christians become believers without really understanding what the phrase means: trusting and committing to Jesus for life.

Many believers didn't know what they signed up for when they became Christians. A lack of understanding can put us in a position to miss a powerful and important step, and it can blind us once we do become Christians. When we say something, we are trusting that what we are saying is true and we are willing to commit to it. "The tongue has the power of life and death, and those who love it will eat its fruit" (Proverbs 18:21 NIV). The words that come out of our mouths are important to our salvation. The tongue, or our words, can give us life and death.

The Christian journey is like signing up for a beautiful marriage. Marriage is a metaphor for the meaning of "Jesus is Lord." For a relationship to enter marriage, it must first accomplish trust and commitment. Human relationships take time to build, because we are sinful and have a lot of junk in our lives. Two flawed people have to trust God and follow His ways to make it in marriage. God is flawless; therefore, the problem cannot be with God. Dating is a must for couples because of their flaws, but there is no dating with God because He is perfect. When we acknowledge Jesus as Lord, we declare that God is a perfect creator whom we can trust and commit to right away.

Believing in our heart that "Jesus is Lord" also has a powerful, misunderstood meaning. Many people say they believe, but it has become so normal to do so that it's lost its meaning. The true spiritual meaning of belief is a continuous act of obedience. It's sad how we apply "belief" to God without knowing the word's meaning.

Belief is the third stage to understanding salvation. First, the declaration, "Jesus is Lord," leads to complete trust in God; second, the same declaration reveals lifelong commitment to God; and third is belief, which is continuous obedience to the word of God. When we invite Jesus into our hearts, it is the biggest and the most significant decision of our lives. It is irresponsible to make the choice based off of our emotions.

The fourth awareness is accepting that God raised Jesus from the dead, making Him ruler over death and Hell. Belief (consistent obedience) is a declaration, and it ties into the fourth step: believing in the power of resurrection. Resurrection is all about getting back up and growing with the help of Jesus. Before Jesus was resurrected, humanity had a hard time growing and returning to God. People needed a savior and a Holy Spirit to live in their lives and strengthen them in good times and bad. Relying on God's strength is all about activating the power of the resurrection. Walking in God's truth and being led by the Holy Spirit are key to the power of resurrection and transformation.

"Yet to all who did receive him, to those who believed in his name, he gave the right to become children of God" (John 1:12 NIV). When people have children, they make rules to govern over them. When children break the rules, parents discipline them. Ironically, God does the same thing with us, and some people don't like that. Accepting Jesus into your heart is a lifelong commitment to following Him. Believing in His name is a step toward a life of obedience as His child. When we fall, Jesus is right there to pick us up, the Holy Spirit is living in us to guide us, and God is always there to protect us. If we want children to accept our rules, we must first be an example of Christ. Parents are human and make mistakes, and that is why they need to imitate the perfect savior's action. To be children of God, we must run to God and abide by His word and law. We do not need to live by our strength but by the power and resurrection of Jesus Christ.

Once people accept Jesus, they need the church's help to continue the relationship. The church is a place where people are sure of their faith, because it's the house of the Lord. The church does not replace the gifts of God or the guidance of the Holy Spirit, but it does create a safe environment. The church is home for many Christians. The church consists of people who believe in Jesus Christ and are collectively called the body of Christ. Every believer needs a home to feel confident and secure. In our homes, we feel comfortable enough to be ourselves, and the church is set up to be the same. To feel at home in the house of the Lord, we must be sure of our faith. Many Christians become believers and then turn back to their old lifestyles. They lose their faith because of uncertainty.

Worship, sermons, and church programs are a support system for faith assurance. "On that day you will realize that I am in my Father, and you are in me, and I am in you" (John 14:20 NIV). Salvation is eternal because of Jesus Christ, who lives in us now and forever as a result of the Holy Spirit. Many sermons and Bible studies frustrate believers in their faith rather than assure them. Christians are children of God, and new Christians are infants. Infants need to build trust with their parents. In the same way, new Christians need to build assurance in their faith.

The norm is that Jesus is just a gift, but He is actually a continuous and eternal reward. The greatest gift Jesus continues with the work of the Holy Spirit. The beauty of being a Christian must be reflected in church, worship, sermons, and our lives.

A majority of Christians have the Holy-Spirit residing inside of them, but they always lose the battle against the devil. Whenever a soldier goes to war, he or she carries a weapon. Every soldier willing to fight and die knows how to use a weapon. Salvation blesses us with great weapons that we must learn how to use. To kill the enemy, the weapon must be used correctly. The more I realize that Christ is in me, the more I submit and trust Him. Understanding the power of God is to unleash the weapons of righteousness, holiness, obedience, and submission to God.

Being an early childhood teacher, I see children's joy and excitement when they are with their parents. Their moms and dads mean the world to them. Children are more confident and secure when they have loving, present parents, just like Christians are more confident and secure when they know that Jesus Christ lives in them.

Humanity's greatest fear is being alone, and it is the devil's greatest weapon. I trust God more and more because I know He lives in me. Realization is a powerful weapon in our Christian faith and understanding. Many people lose their lives before they realize their potential. We defeat fear when we recognize that the King of Glory lives in us.

Every Christian sins, but not all are sure that their sins are forgiven through Jesus Christ. "When you were dead in your sins and in the uncircumcision of your flesh, God made you alive with Christ. He forgave us all our sins, having canceled the charge of our legal indebtedness, which stood against us and condemned us; he has taken it away, nailing it to the cross" (Colossians 2:13-14 NIV). Forgiveness is a gift, and it assures our faith. Everyone is responsible for their sin, but for thousands of years that responsibility was too hard and overwhelming for individuals who believed in God. Sin consumed mankind and separated it from God, but then Jesus Christ came and reunited humanity with God, setting it free from the bondage of sin.

"I write these things to you who believe in the name of the Son of God so that you may know that you have eternal life" (1 John 5:13 NIV). Life is not about having the best things on Earth. When we focus on earthly things, we forget about eternal life. We have confidence and safety because we know that our ending is secure. Humans are so busy with wanting more blessings that they forget to enjoy the beauty of eternal life here on Earth. Eternal life is a guarantee, and it is set up for humanity to enjoy the promise on Earth as well. Life on earth is temporary, and one day when we die, we will go home to live with Jesus forever. Our belief in Jesus Christ and acceptance of Him as our savior is eternal. We can live our lives with confidence because of the promise of eternal life in Jesus Christ.

Accepting Jesus into our lives was the best decision we ever made. Married people look back at their wedding day to remember happy moments. In that same way, we must look back at the day we accepted Christ and be grateful. Looking back reminds us of God's promise and eternal love, grace, and mercy. When people know that their end is secure, they start to live as a winner, but many Christians live in defeat, because they don't think about God's promise. But His promise is alive and well, and we need to hang on to it.

REFERENCE

Child Abuse Statistics. (n.d.). Retrieved from https://www.childhelp.org/child-abuse-statistics/.

Munroe, M. (2014). *Power of character in leadership: How values, morals, ethics, and principles affect leaders.* New Kensington, PA: Whitaker House.

Lencioni, P. (2002). *The five dysfunctions of a team: A leadership fable.* San Francisco, CA:

U.S. Census Bureau. (2018, August 01). Newsroom. Retrieved from https://www.census.gov/newsroom/stories/2018/world-population.html

Printed in the United States
By Bookmasters